Secrets of

ALEXANDER
TECHNIQUE

D1512845

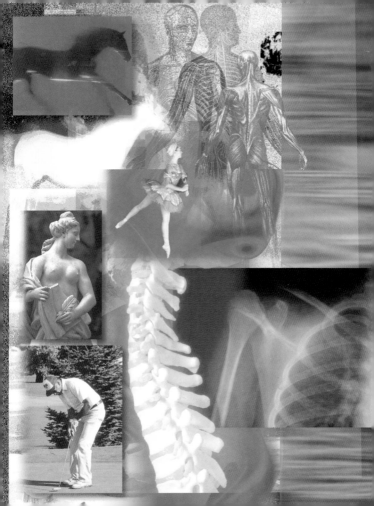

Secrets of
ALEXANDER TECHNIQUE

ROBERT MACDONALD
AND CARO NESS

EVERGREEN

EVERGREEN is an imprint of TASCHEN GmbH

© 2006 TASCHEN GmbH
Hohenzollernring 53, D-50672 Köln
www.taschen.com

This book was conceived, designed and produced by
THE IVY PRESS LIMITED,
The Old Candlemakers,
Lewes. East Sussex BN7 2NZ
Art director *Peter Bridgewater*
Editorial director *Sophie Collins*
Designers *Kevin Knight, Jane Lanaway*
Editor *Rowan Davies*
Picture researcher *Liz Eddison*
Photography *Guy Ryecart*
Illustrations *Sarah Young, Ivan Hissey, Michael Courtney*
Three-dimensional models *Mark Jamieson*
Copyright © The Ivy Press Limited, 2001

All rights reserved. No part of this publication may be reproduced,
stored in a retrieval system, or transmitted in any form or by any means,
electronic, mechanical, photocopying, recording, or otherwise,
without the prior written permission of the copyright owner.

Printed in China

ISBN-13: 978-3-8228-5647-5
ISBN-10: 3-8228-5647-9

Note from the publisher
Although every effort has been
made to ensure that the information presented
in this book is correct, the author and
publisher cannot be held responsible for any
injuries which may arise.

CONTENTS

HOW TO USE THIS BOOK

This book comprises four sections. The first part introduces Frederick Matthias Alexander and his work. The second teaches you about body structure and functions and encourages you to begin applying the principles of inhibition and direction to your life. The third section covers activities such as sitting, lying down, writing, and running, encouraging you to apply the procedures you have learned with your teacher in an Alexander Lesson. The final section broadens your horizons by relating the use of conscious control to specific situations and skills.

Please Note

While the information presented within the pages of this book will be useful to anybody who is considering taking a course of lessons in the Alexander Technique, it is important to realise that one can really only undertake training in the Technique under the guidance of a qualified teacher. The information in this book is not a substitute for such instruction. Please see pages 218–219 for guidance on finding a teacher.

EARLY DISCOVERIES

When Alexander first began to suffer from hoarseness and to lose his voice, he consulted doctors and voice teachers, but the problem continued. Prior to a particularly important recital, his doctor suggested that he rest his voice completely for the two weeks leading up to the performance. Alexander followed this advice and his voice worked well at the beginning of the show, but as the performance continued he became hoarser and eventually lost his voice completely. Since the problem did not occur until he came to use his voice, Alexander concluded that it must be caused by something that he was doing when he spoke.

By observing himself reciting in front of mirrors, he noticed a pattern of stiffening his neck and retracting his head, depressing his larynx, and sucking breath in through his mouth. This unconscious habit was so ingrained that it took him many years to learn how to prevent it and allow a freer way of speaking to take place. Not only did his voice recover completely, but his general health improved dramatically.

Early learning
Alexander grabs a hold of his golden wheat. Young children have a natural ease of movement.

Sitting comfortably
Alexander sitting in to East garden with his dog.

Helping hands
Alexander's strong, skeleton and sensitive hand encourage a free and balanced posture.

The basics
The first part of the book outlines Alexander's life and his practical theories, such as the importance of the primary control and conscious inhibition and direction.

MOVEMENT

MOVEMENT The coordinated energy of a cat running at full speed, the elegance of a horse jumping, or the alert stillness of a lion stalking its prey, are all reminders of the extraordinary beauty and freedom of animal movement. Human movement is more complicated. Because the spine lengthens vertically, and you move in the horizontal, the spine can become shortened. Animals keep their spines lengthened whatever the direction of what is being generated by their limbs. When they are frightened, they retract their heads and shorten their spines. This is always in preparation for action. When the frightening stimulus ceases, the animal recovers its equilibrium. This is shown by a release of the neck and a return to normal breathing. Humans do not necessarily recover as quickly and are capable of holding on to a state of fear or defeat, expressed in a protest attitude, long after a stimulus goes.

Head leads body
In animal movement, the head and the body move in a horizontal line.

In flight
When the head leads, the animal can relax at ease, as shown by the freeze-frame photo of a horse leaping.

Moving forwards
All umbrellas move with the head leading the body. In humans, the head leads the spine vertically or makes the the body in motion forwards.

Freedom in action
Man's superior inheritance is this notorious intelligence which enables him to adapt to a changing world.

Beginnings
The second section, First Steps, allows you to appreciate that your birthright is an inbuilt capacity for balance, ease, and grace in movement.

Practice
The third, and longest, section introduces you to the Alexander procedures, which encourage a deeper awareness of how the mind and body work together.

SQUATTING

SQUATTING Follow the simple basics of letting your head go forwards, hips go backwards, and knees go forwards, and see how far you can go. If you really want to try and get down to the floor, hold on to something fixed, such as a banister and counterbalance yourself against this reliable anchor. Do not repeat the exercise too many times; do not try to get further than you can, and remember that the end is just as important as the beginning. Returning to a standing position requires that you let your head go forwards and up, and you are careful not to hold your breath or help with your arms.

1 Stand with your feet slightly wider than your hips. Before you lower yourself to the ground, pause to allow your neck to be free so that your spine can lengthen.

2 Begin to lower yourself towards the ground by letting your head and forwards, your pelvis drops down, and your knees release forwards.

Hips free to allow head to seek back.

Knees free to go forwards

3 Continue to let your head go forwards and up, your pelvis back and down, and your knees forwards over your feet.

Neck relaxed

4 Release your knee head to nod forwards, let your pelvis drop away from your head. In this position, place on a relaxed stretch as the muscles throughout your body.

Feet flat on floor

Pregnancy and Childbirth

Feeling the strain
The growing foetus passes on the 'main' tags, and other internal organs, often causing digestive problems or breathing difficulties.

During pregnancy, a woman's body undergoes a bewildering number of physical and psychological changes. As hormones flood through her, affecting her emotional state, her body is accommodating the foetus within. As the baby grows, the increased weight of

the foetus shifts her centre of balance. The woman's usual instinct is to lean back from the waist to compensate for the extra weight she has to carry. In doing this, she puts untold pressure on the lower back and sacrum, resulting in chronic back pain.

An Alexander teacher will show a pregnant woman how to expand her torso and release pressure from the spinal area, redistributing the baby's weight through her body. This protects the back and alleviates restriction of the internal organs, allowing her to breathe freely. The weight of the baby also affects the woman's range and ease of movement. Simple everyday tasks such as bending, lifting, carrying, standing, and sitting become increasingly difficult or uncomfortable. The woman, a pregnant woman begins tensions in her Alexander technique, the better: it takes time to replace ingrained patterns of muscular tension. Having learnt to exercise conscious control over posture

and movement, the woman can apply this skill to her daily life and also, crucially, prepare for childbirth itself.

Childbirth
For most women, the instinctive response to pain is to tense the whole body and hold the breath, and this is compounded by the expectation of pain with each contraction, leading to anxiety. Anxiety, in turn, releases all the wrong hormones and may halt or delay the birthing process. Similarly, the use of painkilling drugs confuses the body's signals and may result in the need for medical intervention.

The Whispered "Ah" exercise is beneficial when a contraction is due. Alexander's instruction for dealing with anxiety was to think of something funny and smile. The act of smiling releases tension in the jaw and face, ensuring the airways dilate to secrete saliva. Saliva sends a message to the brain that all is well and there is no need for anxiety.

Achievement
The final section, Self Mastery, helps you to utilize two powerful resources – self-awareness and personal choice – and employ them for everyday tasks, exercise, work, and for general wellbeing.

Introduction

F. M. Alexander
Alexander was born in Tasmania in 1869, and moved to London when he was 34. He died in 1955.

The Alexander Technique is an important addition to man's resources of self-awareness and personal education. Established by Frederick Matthias Alexander at the turn of the last century, the Alexander Technique is widely recognized in medical, educational, theatrical, and musical circles as a reliable and effective method of self-help and self-mastery. The Alexander Technique helps you to achieve good posture, freedom of movement, easy breathing, confidence, and general wellbeing, while relieving back pain, neck pain, and general stiffness. It enables you to feel calmer, think more clearly, and work more efficiently.

These benefits are not achieved by a system of exercises, but through a thought process that encourages increased awareness of how your habits of muscular tension restrict activity. Standing naturally, breathing easily, and moving gracefully were once activities that you took for granted, but now they are more difficult. Lessons in the Alexander Technique help you to recognize and prevent the effort that interferes with your ability to stand easily at your full height, with good balance and with minimum effort. It is not so much a "how to do it" technique, but a "how to stop what is stopping you" technique. This awareness serves as a basis for growth and development on all levels and in all spheres of life and enables your natural endowment of poise, grace, inner calm, and general alertness to become a real possibility.

What your posture reveals

Your posture is an expression of you, reflecting what you think and feel – your fears, anxieties, and doubts; your joys, dreams, and successes. It mirrors your reactions and inner responses to life and has a profound effect on your whole mind–body–self. The Alexander Technique helps you to make sense of this interconnection, gives you the choice over how you respond, and invites you to harness the power of your conscious mind.

The principles discussed in the early part of this book grew directly out of Alexander's own practical experience. He made certain observations and then he formalized his ideas and developed the concepts of the Technique. Like any scientific principle, it has been proved to work by repeated experiments over the last hundred years. As you read this book, stop and observe yourself as you try to apply these principles throughout your daily life. Even better, contact an Alexander teacher who can help you in the voyage of self-discovery.

F. M. ALEXANDER

Frederick Matthias Alexander was born in Tasmania in 1869, the son of a farmer. His ambition was to become an actor and he launched himself on a promising career as a solo performer. In the mid-1890s he began to experience vocal difficulties, which doctors were unable to diagnose. Observing himself in mirrors, he concluded that his condition derived from a faulty use of the postural mechanism, and that such misuse was responsible for many of mankind's ills in the stressful modern world. In *The Use of the Self* (1932) he described this process of self-discovery and the Technique he evolved to help himself and others overcome their bad habits.

Alexander: A Profile

At the age of 20, Alexander went to Melbourne in Australia where he began practising his new Technique. In 1899, he moved to Sydney where he became director of the Sydney Dramatic and Operatic Conservatorium. He described his method as one of "basically changing and controlling reaction". His Technique helped many cases that had confounded doctors and, armed with recommendations from leading Australian physicians, he set out in 1904, when he was 34, for London, England. Within a few years, he had established a large and fashionable practice there. His pupils included the playwright George Bernard Shaw, the actors Sir Henry Irving and Lily Langtree, and the imperial administrator Lord Lytton. He published his first book on the Technique, called *Man's Supreme Inheritance*, in 1910. The outbreak of war in 1914 led to the decline of his practice, so he moved to America where he won many new supporters, notably the great educationalist John Dewey.

Teaching children
Alexander set up a school where children were taught according to his principles. Here he works with a pupil.

Spreading the word

Back in England after the war, Alexander resumed his practice. Many physicians were allies, as well as influential figures such as the politician Stafford Cripps, and the novelist Aldous Huxley. He published three further books – *Constructive Conscious Control of the Individual*, *The Use of the Self*, and *The Universal Constant in Living*, and set up a school to educate children according to his principles, and

inaugurated a course for training
Alexander teachers. His later years
were clouded by a libel action against
the South African government, which
published a magazine in which he was
accused of being a charlatan.

Anxiety over this action led to
Alexander suffering a mild stroke in
1947, but the Technique was
vindicated by a resounding victory in
the courts. Many of the people who he
had helped over the years rallied to
give convincing evidence for his
defence. Alexander recovered fully and
died in London in 1955, aged 86. To
the last, he continued to run the training
course, give private lessons, lead an
active life, and indulge his love of food,
wine, and horse racing.

After his death, the management of
the training course fell to his pupil,
Walter Carrington, who, with his wife
Dilys, continues his work in London. This
school is now called The Constructive
Teaching Centre and is a focal point for
the international community of
Alexander teachers.

EARLY DISCOVERIES

When Alexander first began to suffer from hoarseness and to lose his voice, he consulted doctors and voice teachers, but the problem continued. Prior to a particularly important recital, his doctor suggested that he rest his voice completely for the two weeks leading up to the performance. Alexander followed this advice and his voice worked well at the beginning of the show, but as the performance continued, he became hoarse and eventually lost his voice completely. Since the problem did not occur until he came to use his voice, Alexander concluded that it must be caused by something that he was doing when he spoke.

By observing himself reciting in front of mirrors, he noticed a pattern of stiffening his neck and retracting his head, depressing his larynx, and sucking breath in through his mouth. This unconscious habit was so ingrained that it took him many years to learn how to prevent it and allow a freer way of speaking to take place. Not only did his voice recover completely, but his general health improved dramatically.

Early learning
Alexander guides a pupil at his London school. Young children have a natural ease of movement.

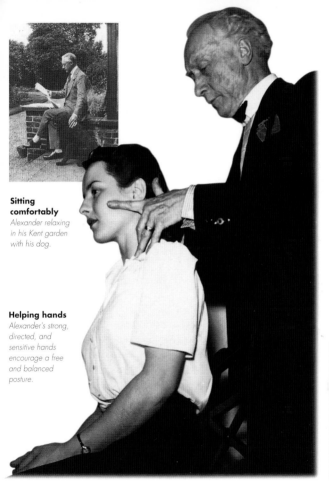

Sitting comfortably
Alexander relaxing in his Kent garden with his dog.

Helping hands
Alexander's strong, directed, and sensitive hands encourage a free and balanced posture.

Primary Control

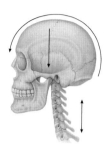

Balance of the head
Control of the head–neck–back relationship is fundamental to good use of the body.

The primary control is the specific relationship between the head, neck, and back, which influences the coordination of the whole of the rest of the body. By observing his movements in a mirror, Alexander discovered that he habitually stiffened his neck, retracted his head, and shortened and narrowed his back. This indirectly led to his constricting his throat and sucking in breath through his mouth. Contracting the head, neck, and back region led to the tightening of his

throat and persistent loss of voice. When he did not interfere with the head, neck, and back, he regained full use of his voice. The added bonus was that his general health improved.

The power of the head and neck

Alexander made a fundamental discovery about human physiology. He recognized that the maintenance of the tone of his neck muscles, and the position of his head relative to the other parts of his body, was a primary requirement for the efficient use of the body. The noted anthropologist Raymond Dart endorsed this discovery by saying that it is a basic biological fact that the position of the head to the neck is of primary importance in human posture and movement.

Using primary control

Many of your bodily functions, such as breathing, circulation, and digestion, are determined by how well you are using your primary control. It determines coordination, grace and the efficiency of all movement. The continuing influence of your ability to facilitate the primary control over general functioning is a foundation for health and wellbeing. You may be unaware of the extent to which you interfere with the use of your primary control. Alexander's discovery goes beyond what he observed in himself. It is a general principle that applies to the whole question of the widespread decline in efficient posture, health, and wellbeing.

Alexander worked out a method whereby the primary control could be established as a way of working. By applying the processes of inhibition and formulating the direction to "Let the neck be free so that the head can go forward and up and the back can lengthen and widen", he synthesized a method whereby the mechanism which influences the subtle freedom and dynamic relationship between the head–neck–back and the breathing could work more efficiently.

MIND–BODY CONNECTION

Each time you respond to a stimulus, your mind and body are acting together. Lessons in the Alexander Technique help you to appreciate how fundamental this relationship is. Whether you are happy or sad, interested or bored, joyful or angry, confident or frightened, patient or impatient, positive or negative, these responses are expressed in the way you stand and breathe.

Standing easily

Young people are naturally capable of maintaining an alert stillness. This becomes more difficult as we get older.

Sitting comfortably

Because of the deep connection between your reaction and the functioning of the postural mechanisms, your shape may be defined by your overall experience and response to life.

The control freak
Over-confidence, fixed opinions and self-assurance can result in a braced posture.

The challenger
A tendency to react too quickly to every stimulus leads to anger and aggression.

The underdog
The tendency to take all stimuli as self-criticism leads to depression.

Identifying Habits

Habitual response
Some habits provide helpful ways of dealing with situations; others are counterproductive.

Habits are set patterns of physical actions or ways of behaving. Many of our habits are learnt responses that have become settled and automatic because we keep repeating them time after time. Habits have various guises: they can crop up in a pattern of thought, a method of doing something, or the way you perform an action. The Alexander Technique helps you to gain particular insight into how you do the things that you do.

Over-reaction

Through his observations, Alexander became aware of his tendency to over-react when he needed to speak. Indeed, any situation that required action made him behave in a similar way. This over-reaction was expressed by tightening his neck muscles, pulling his head back and down, and over-tightening the muscles in the front of his body, which shortened him in stature. Alexander realized that this pattern was the basis of all his responses. His subsequent work as a teacher of the Technique confirmed that it was a universal pattern and most people tended to over-react in a similar way.

This habit is sometimes subtle and imperceptible, but over time it shapes you and can affect your health and wellbeing. Over the years, the natural functioning of balance, posture, and breathing can be impaired and result in unwelcome and detrimental wear and tear on the body. This can lead to degeneration and, in severe cases, potential disease.

End-gaining

End-gaining refers to a tendency to focus on the end result while disregarding the process that you use to achieve that end. Alexander believed that the habit of end-gaining was the greatest impediment to changing behaviour. Getting good results is important, but often incorrect effort means that you undermine your best intentions and limit yourself.

Channelling inner drives

When you consider that sometimes, when we try to relax, we become more tense in the process, the absurdity of end-gaining is apparent. The tendency is rooted in our survival response, expressed in the desire to get things right and the fear of getting things wrong. In this sense, many habits grow from instinctive drives.

The Alexander Technique helps you to form an ongoing relationship to these forces within, and provides a means whereby they can be channelled in a way that is more beneficial.

SENSORY APPRECIATION

If we repeat an action often enough, even if it is difficult or harmful at first, it eventually feels natural. It feels right simply because we have become used to it. After a while it begins to feel normal to be shortened, stiffened and generally pulled down. Alexander referred to this as unreliable sensory appreciation. When he watched himself reciting in front of the mirror, he was surprised to see that he was retracting his head and shortening his stature. What he saw himself doing and what he felt he was doing were not the same thing.

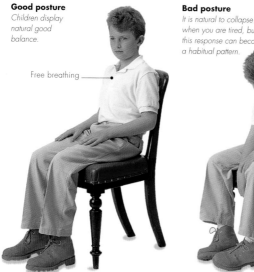

Good posture

Children display natural good balance.

Free breathing

Bad posture

It is natural to collapse when you are tired, but this response can become a habitual pattern.

Restricted breathing

Observing reaction
When Alexander recited in front of the mirror, he discovered that he was tightening his body without noticing. He called this faulty sensory appreciation. After they qualify, Alexander teachers continue to refine their sensory appreciation. Try working in front of a mirror to see whether you are tensing parts of your body without being aware of it.

Released neck

Conscious Inhibition

Free choice
Take a moment to assess the level of muscular tension in your body before you carry out any action.

How often have you heard the words, "Why don't you think before you speak?", or "Take your time!", or "More haste, less speed!" You are constantly receiving stimuli from the outside world. At the same time, you are receiving countless internal messages. You may feel that you sometimes respond to these external stimuli automatically in ways that, on reflection, strike you as unnecessary, inappropriate, or even self-destructive.

Perhaps you over-prepare for action – even the very thought of doing something stimulates an unnecessary increase in muscular tension. Your past experience, and what you have got used to doing, have set up physiological programs which are stored in the brain. All the unnecessary tensions that you make are retained as part of that pattern.

Breaking habits

The word "inhibition" means "to stop". The process of stopping before you act gives you the chance to allow your balance, freedom of movement, and general wellbeing to function better. However, if you are going to allow this natural ease to operate, it is first necessary to be aware that your habitual response tends to prevail. Inhibition gives you the chance to prevent these unwanted reactions, by creating a gap between the stimulus and the response. This gap provides the time and the space needed for the desired response to happen. When you suspend your response to stimuli for a millisecond and allow your conscious, reasoned choice to intervene, you can break the stranglehold that habits have over you and give yourself more freedom to choose your response.

Dealing with extra stress

If you are in a difficult situation or feeling emotionally bruised, it is understandable that you tense up. But if you apply the inhibitory process you can stop this reaction and let yourself experience your situation and learn from it. You can only do this if you allow yourself enough time to stop in order to facilitate change. You may believe that stopping to think about your response is going to slow you down, but you will soon find that it is a natural process which saves you time by avoiding thoughtless action and wasted effort.

Ready to Perform

Alexander's experience as a stage performer gave him insight into human reaction.

CONSCIOUS INHIBITION

The inhibitory process is the basis for learning how to take action. It is not the same as suppression. You are asked to look clearly at what you are doing, examining your performance as a whole, not just in terms of what must be done to achieve your goal, but what it is you are doing that prevents a successful outcome. What are the tensions that you are creating that block your freedom in activity? You have a better chance of responding freely and clearly by stopping before you act. The inhibitory process is the key to successful performance – stop and say "No" or "No, I don't have to do it in my usual way". This is to help you to address the problems caused by constantly responding too quickly or trying too hard to get things right. By suspending action, excessive or unnecessary effort can be prevented.

Wu Wei
This shows the Chinese characters for the concept of "non-doing".

Animal wisdom
When stalking prey, animals know that if they make a move too soon, the prey will escape.

Tension build-up

Today, many people's work and home lives put their time under constant pressure, but we still struggle to meet impossible schedules.

Daily learning

Our families provide an ongoing stimulus not to over-react.

27

A Consciously Directed Self

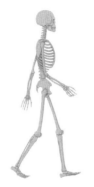

Efficient movement
If you can prevent the wrong thing happening, the right thing does "do itself".

Directions are the thoughts that encourage your body to lengthen and widen in stature. Being able to give directions is a delicate process. Often the wish for something to happen causes you to increase muscular tension. Directions are conscious acts of intention and refer to your capacity to make choices and to act on them.

Alexander found that when he stiffened his neck, retracted his head, and shortened and narrowed his body, he interfered with his vocal functioning. He lost his voice as a result of the incorrect use of his body through misdirection. He found that when he was lengthening and widening throughout his body, he created the conditions that enabled his voice to work freely, effectively and expressively. He formulated the directions: "Let the neck be free, so that the head can go forward and up, so that the spine can lengthen and back can widen." These precise commands helped to bring about the correct working of the primary control.

Preventive awareness

The directions used in the Alexander Technique are largely preventive instructions. We have all experienced the tendency, when standing and moving, to over-tighten muscles generally throughout the body,

particularly the neck and the strong muscles down the front of the body. These habitual patterns have to be recognized before you can escape them, and avoided in such a way that tension is not increased. When you think about standing up straight, it is not uncommon to over-tighten your muscles in order to achieve the upright posture you imagine it to be.

Sensitive thinking

When giving directions, it is not just a matter of where you wish your body to go, but of preventing the habits that pull you down. It is no use activating old habits of tensing whilst using the directions to move differently in space. Habits of muscular tension and the end-gaining tendency are always ready to come into play. When the directions happen properly, it is as if they "do themselves". A clear and subtle form of sensitive thinking is required to send directions effectively.

Finding your position
A compass is an invaluable aid when navigating. In the same way, if your thoughts are clear, the correct postural response will follow.

DIRECTED THOUGHT
As you begin practising your directions, you will notice that subtle but dramatic changes begin to happen in you and your responses. By developing the necessary skill and sensitivity to influence your posture through directions, the ability to communicate with the roots of your behaviour is improved in general. Although you need to be clear about what is wanted and needed, any instructions must be given in such a way that the appropriate postural response can take care of itself. The thought process should allow you to remain open to feedback from your body. Sometimes you will find that you are trying too hard and unconsciously blocking yourself.

Taking aim
Thought, balance, strength, and free direction lead to a successful outcome.

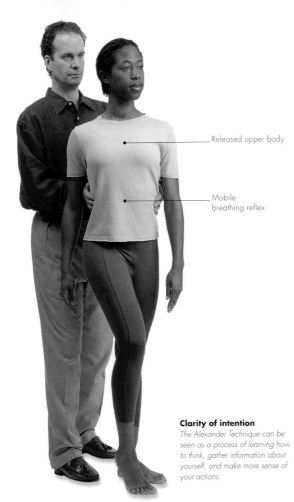

Released upper body

Mobile
breathing reflex

Clarity of intention

*The Alexander Technique can be
seen as a process of learning how
to think, gather information about
yourself, and make more sense of
your actions.*

Using Conscious Control

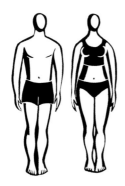

Making choices

Lessons in the Alexander Technique encourage you to use thought and awareness during activity.

The fear of getting things wrong can cause you to focus on the end result at the expense of how you are performing. The Alexander Technique encourages you to balance your focus between what is being done and how you are doing it, and to pay more attention to the process that you use. It asks you to experience the fact that many of your intentions and actions are easily translated into muscular tension. The Alexander Technique enables you to bring these tensions into conscious awareness and to focus on how to ensure the free working of the primary control before, during, and after action.

We are living in the time of the 30-second soundbite and under the constant expectation that everything must be done more and more quickly. Redundancy, temporary contracts, early retirement, and the fear of replacement or failure all create psychological pressures to get everything right. Under such stress, we tend to try even harder.

What's the rush?

If you constantly do things quickly, you are habitually activating the areas of the brain that are designed to deal with emergency situations. Overstimulating your fight or flight response is not an ideal way of doing things. Habitual end-gaining may involve a constant activation of the fight or flight response which, after a while, becomes stressful and unhealthy. When it becomes so deeply ingrained that you forget how to recover your equilibrium, then you are in serious trouble.

Instigating conscious control

The tendency to prefer end-gaining over the means you use to get to the goal comes from your belief about the best way to get results (for instance the thought that the "end" justifies the "means"), and from the expectation that a lot of effort is required to achieve any task. This feeling will be rooted in your sensory appreciation, a sense based on your muscular awareness and past experience of doing things. Changing your habitual end-gaining tendency to a conscious control of the means you use (described by Alexander as "the means-whereby") will require a clear consideration of how you want to work, an ability to inhibit the old muscular response associated with your usual way of performing, and conscious direction, to ensure the free working of the primary control during activity.

THINKING IN ACTIVITY

Before you perform any action, it is advisable to develop a systematic approach. By considering how you are going to do it, you can save yourself a lot of trouble. By saying "No" to over-preparation you allow areas of excess tension, such as the neck, shoulders, front of the body, lower back, legs, and feet to release. Then you can give directions, such as: "I would like my head to go forwards and up, so my spine can lengthen, my back can widen, and my pelvis can drop so that my legs are free to release out of my lower back."

1 *Before you move, pause for a moment, and release your tendency to over-prepare for movement. Allow your neck to be free, your spine to lengthen, and your back to widen.*

2 *Take a step back with your left foot and transfer your weight down through that foot. Your right shoulder will automatically rotate back as your left shoulder comes forwards. Breathe out through your mouth and allow the breath to return through your nose.*

3 Breathe out as you move forward. Allow your right shoulder to rotate forward as you step forwards with your left foot.

4 Allowing your neck to be free, so that your spine can lengthen, releasing the natural rotating movements of your torso, which carries you forwards with rhythm and energy.

Alexander's Writings

Published works
The Use of the Self,
F. M. Alexander's third publication.

In his first book, *Man's Supreme Inheritance* (1910), Alexander argued that whilst our ancestors displayed good instinctual body use, these same instincts did not equip us for the rapid changes of civilization, resulting in possible habitual misuse of our bodies. Recognizing mind–body unity, he proposed that habit could not be confined to physical or mental misuse, but should be seen as a response of the whole self. He maintained that if we study conscious control of ourselves, we will recognize true body poise, inhibit habitual misuse, direct the body into an efficient posture, and maintain improved function at all times. Our "supreme inheritance" is the possibility of moving from unconscious misuse and unreliable sensory appreciation to conscious control of ourselves.

In *Constructive Conscious Control of the Individual* (1924), Alexander reasoned that if our sensory appreciation is unreliable, an efficient use of the body is compromised. He introduced the term "end-gaining" to describe the way that we proceed directly to a desired end without thinking, resulting in an unsatisfactory use of ourselves. He insisted that it is necessary to pay close attention to the process of achieving a desired end, and called this "the means-whereby". By recognizing our faulty sensory appreciation, we begin to eliminate end-gaining and attempt to consciously direct our effort.

In his third book, *The Use of the Self* (1931), Alexander described the evolution of his Technique in detail. He showed how use influences functioning, underlining the importance of the primary control. He reasoned that misdirection is associated with unreliable sensory appreciation and instinctive misuse, but by learning the technique of conscious inhibition, we redirect stature and improve general performance. He emphasized that his Technique did not treat specific symptoms but established a better use of the whole self.

Use affects function

In *The Universal Constant in Living* (1941), Alexander demonstrated how use or misuse can exert a "constant" influence over general performance and reaction. Exercise of any kind can aggravate unreliable sensory appreciation, since it requires the use of the very sensory processes that need correction. Alexander encouraged his pupils to think before acting: to inhibit their response to any stimulus. In doing so, they experienced an improved, more upright stature accompanied by increased freedom of movement, health, and general wellbeing.

FIRST STEPS

In this section you will learn about yourself, the structure of your body, and how it functions. You will begin to appreciate that you have an inbuilt capacity for balance, ease, and grace in movement. You will begin to understand your natural breathing rhythms and your inspiration. You will recognize that there are habits that over-ride your finely tuned mechanisms of balance and posture, leading to constriction, excessive effort, fatigue, breathlessness, and poor co-ordination. ↄ As you put together this new map of yourself and start to apply the basic principles of inhibition and direction, you will begin to understand that your psychophysical balance and wellbeing are intimately connected with the choices you make.

Learning to Work with Gravity

Counteracting gravity
The Alexander Technique shows you how to deal with gravity efficiently.

Sometimes it is argued that the human muscular and skeletal system is poorly designed for standing upright, and that many of the postural and functional problems that human beings experience are due to an inherent structural problem. On the other hand, there is another view that maintains that gravity poses a dilemma when you use your body inefficiently – it is the way humans use themselves that is the problem, not their design. When you observe the natural world, you see all living things counteract the downward force of gravity in a way that appears to be natural and effortless. Your experience of gravity may be of a force that drags you down, or perhaps you feel that somehow the field of gravity helps you to stand tall. Lessons in the Alexander Technique show you how to deal with gravity in an efficient way.

Standing tall

Alexander reasoned that pulling his head back and down shortened his stature and interfered with the free functioning of his postural mechanisms. The free working of these mechanisms orientates the body away from the ground. When you stand at your full height, the body is organized around the perpendicular, so there is very little weight in front or behind your central axis for gravity to get hold of. In this situation, gravity functions to your advantage and helps you to stand; the forward nod of the head activates a response from the highly efficient postural muscles in the back. Through lessons in the Alexander Technique, people come to understand that the human body is beautifully designed to deal with gravity.

Fear of falling

Your head is a very delicate structure and your balance operates to ensure that your head does not hit the ground. Fear of falling is part of a basic survival mechanism, which ensures that you do not fall down.

When the balance of your head on the neck is not efficient, your senses register that you are in danger and your muscles tighten to save you. This action develops into a vicious circle whereby the more you are in danger of falling, the more effort you make to rescue yourself from doing so.

HEAD BALANCE

The head weighs 4.5–7 kilograms (10–15 pounds) and rests on the atlanto-occipital joint. This joint comprises the top two vertebrae of the neck. Being slightly behind the centre of gravity of the skull, the head is inclined to nod forwards. This movement engages the highly efficient postural muscles of the back and brings about a lengthening in stature that enables you to counteract the downward force of gravity naturally. It is like a counterweight which literally allows your spine to lift and lengthen.

Balance

The centre of gravity of the skull is slightly in front of the atlanto-occipital joint so when the muscles of the neck are released, the head is naturally inclined to nod forward.

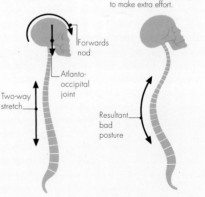

The Dynamics of the Spine

When the head is able to nod forwards freely, the spine has the chance to lengthen up and down.

Stiffening the neck and retracting the head causes excess weight on the top of the spine, requiring the body to make extra effort.

Forwards nod

Atlanto-occipital joint

Two-way stretch

Resultant bad posture

Head balance in action

A free neck allows the head–neck–back relationship to change constantly as the body re-orientates itself during movement.

Standing tall

When the delicate balance of the head on the neck is maintained, a lengthening and widening in stature can occur.

43

Proprioception: Discover Your Sixth Sense

The eyes of the body
Proprioception is your sense of balance, position, and tension in movement.

The five senses are normally described as hearing, sight, smell, taste, and touch. During the middle of the last century, neurophysiologists added a "sixth sense" called proprioception, which refers to our sense of balance, position, and movement in space. This sense relies on input from receptors in the joints and muscles and the organs of balance in the inner ear. Proprioception literally means "to feel within". It is sometimes referred to as "the eyes of the body". Your sixth sense enables you to judge your position and mass in space and be aware of the amount of muscular tension used to keep you there.

Most of the movements that you perform during the day are automatic and do not require any thought. With this ability, you are free to concentrate fully on what you need to do in any given situation or for any task you have to undertake. This is a useful position to be in. However, the disadvantage of this is that it allows you to suppress the feedback that you should be getting from your body when you are over-contracting muscles.

Life involves a constant stimulation of the senses, and, as the pace of life speeds up and you respond to the demands of the external world you may start to disregard the sensory messages from within that are telling you that your muscles are getting tight and fatigued. In the same way, your tensions start to feel normal and even natural, and become deeply embedded in the programming of your body.

Tune in to your sixth sense

Lessons in the Alexander Technique help you to reawaken your sixth sense if it has become blurred. Applying conscious inhibition enables you to pay attention both to the environment and to yourself. It is then possible to receive the messages coming through your sixth sense.

There are great advantages to becoming more aware of your sixth sense. You are more tuned and balanced. You quickly become aware of using your body in a harmful way. This lets you take more control over your stress levels. You become mindful that your posture and your moods are connected and can use this feedback for your continued wellbeing.

MUSCLE FIBRES

There are three different types of muscle fibre in your body: white fibre, red fibre, and postural fibre. The white fibres generate maximum strength for brief periods of time (e.g. sprinting). The red fibres are capable of sustaining effort for longer periods and are therefore used for endurance. The postural fibres are capable of activity at very low levels of contraction for long periods of time, enabling you to support your spine and stand easily. However, through misuse, the postural muscles can atrophy.

Endurance muscles
The red fibres are for endurance and are capable of sustained effort for longer periods of time.

Strength muscles
If these are overused to hold your body up, or are constantly contracting to pull it down, or if you have a collapsed posture, the postural fibres will atrophy.

Muscular balance

It is through your sixth sense that you are aware of the balance between strength, endurance, and postural muscles. It is gravity, not exercise, that stimulates the postural fibres. An Alexander teacher encourages you to release muscular overactivity and helps you to stand in such a way that gravity re-stimulates the postural muscles.

Trapezius muscles

Erector spinae muscles

Multifidus (postural fibres)

Animals Adapting to a Changing Environment

Natural grace

Animals instinctively move in a beautiful way, displaying balance, freedom, and strength.

Animals sometimes display neurotic responses similar to those of humans. In 1925, at London Zoo, 100 baboons, 6 of them female, were placed together in a space 540 metres square with a central concrete mound area surrounded by a moat. Baboons normally live in well-ordered social groups, with a stable dominance hierarchy and unchallenged heterosexual bonds. However, at London Zoo, abnormal tendencies prevailed. Vicious battles for dominance took place between males and within two years 44 baboons were dead.

At this point, the situation stabilized and an uneasy peace prevailed. The zoo introduced 30 more females in an attempt to cheer things up. The remaining males fought over them and within a month 15 of the females had been torn to pieces. By 1930, only 36 males and 5 females had survived.

The human situation

The environment that humans live in is changing rapidly and many social, psychological, and functional problems could be attributed to the difficulty of adapting. Instincts which evolved to deal with a world that we no longer live in still get triggered because they are tried and tested ways of coping. Many stress-related conditions could be the result of the over-activation of instinctive response. When unsuitable responses continually recur, it suggests that a change from an instinctive to a conscious manner of control is required. The animals in the experiment were unable to do this, but human beings, possessed with rational intelligence, can develop and use this skill.

In the case of human behaviour, it is not simply a matter of being natural or returning to an old way of life. It was natural for the baboons in their ancestral environment to live together harmoniously, coping with the occasional conflict. It was equally natural for the baboon to fight for its survival in the cramped conditions at London Zoo. And it is possible, even essential, for humans, living together in a changing and more crowded world, to apply their intelligence to control their instincts and live together in harmony.

Coping with Change

When an animal is unhappy, neurotic responses may emerge. Humans are able to cope with conflict in a conscious way.

MOVEMENT

The co-ordinated energy of a cat running at full speed, the elegance of a horse jumping, or the alert stillness of a lion stalking its prey are all reminders of the extraordinary beauty and freedom of animal movement. Human movement is more complicated. Because the spine lengthens vertically, and you move in the horizontal, the spine can become shortened. Animals keep their spines lengthened whatever the amount of effort being generated by their limbs. When they are frightened, they retract their heads and shorten their spines. This is always a preparation for action. When the frightening stimulus ceases, the animal recovers its equilibrium. This is shown by a release of the neck and a return to normal breathing. Humans do not necessarily recover as quickly and are capable of holding on to a state of fear or defeat, expressed in a postural attitude, long after a stimulus goes.

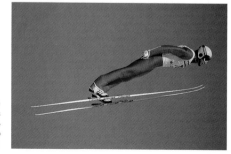

Freedom in action
Man's supreme inheritance is his conscious intelligence which enables him to adapt to a changing world.

In flight

*When the head leads,
the animal can take off
easily, as shown by this
freeze-frame photo of a
mouse leaping.*

Moving forwards

*All vertebrates move with
the head leading the body.
In humans, the head leads
the spine vertically in
order for the body to
move forwards.*

Spirals and Freedom

Discus thrower
This classical statue of a discus
thrower depicts a perfect example
of latent, stored spiral energy.

your cross-pattern reflex, the intrinsic
relationship of your left and right sides
working diagonally through the
arrangement of your muscles. Then you
learn to walk, releasing into the upright
spiral of yourself and beyond yourself.
Every time you need to progress
forwards, you have the chance to wind
up your own movement mechanism, so
without undue effort you can release
easily into movement.

The Star procedure

Experience the spirals in activity with the
Star (from left foot to right hand, and
from right foot to left hand). These
connections are not two-dimensional,
but exist in the deep layers of your
muscles and give the possibility of three-
dimensional movement and release. By
beginning to appreciate the deep
double-helix of yourself and your way of
unfolding into your true size, you can
see how you fit into this natural pattern
of latent, stored energy which at any
moment has the possibility of alert
stillness or controlled movement.

I n the universe, everything comprises,
in one way or another, the spiral
dynamic. Spirals give the world its
possibility for motion. It is the same for
you in your functional organization and
dynamic movement.

When you are in the womb, you are
curled around to fit into the watery sac
that holds you. At the moment of birth,
you twist out of the birth canal. You
begin to crawl forwards, developing

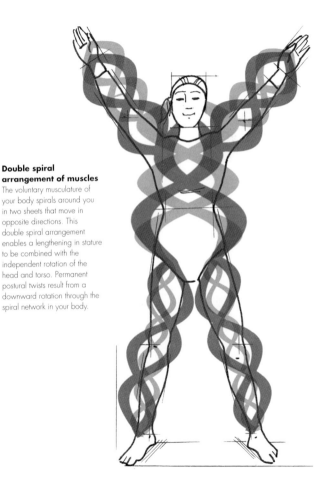

Double spiral arrangement of muscles

The voluntary musculature of your body spirals around you in two sheets that move in opposite directions. This double spiral arrangement enables a lengthening in stature to be combined with the independent rotation of the head and torso. Permanent postural twists result from a downward rotation through the spiral network in your body.

THE HUMAN SKELETON

Every bone in the body, with the exception of the hyoid bone at the base of the tongue, is connected by a joint to at least one other bone. Joints hold the bones together and make movement possible. The skull, on top of the spinal column, is designed for stability, mobility, and the protection of the spinal cord. It consists of 32 vertebrae of bone, through which the spinal cord passes. The chest (or thorax) is made up of 12 pairs of ribs that form a bony cage. Ribs 1–7 get progressively larger, and ribs 8–12 get progressively smaller. The lungs lie enclosed within the airtight thoracic cavity. The structure of the chest cavity is such that it can move in three directions during respiration.

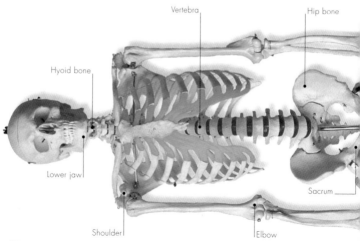

Vertebra

Hip bone

Hyoid bone

Lower jaw

Shoulder

Elbow

Sacrum

Bones

VERTEBRA Each vertebra is separated from the next one by an intervertebral disc made of fibrous cartilage, which acts as a shock-absorbing cushion.

ATLAS/AXIS This pivot joint enables the skull to nod and is crucial to the freedom of our upright posture and our entire movement pattern.

LOWER JAW The lower jaw is hinged for movement by a condyloid joint which allows opening, closing, sliding, chewing, and crushing.

ELBOW The elbow is a combined joint: a hinged joint that allows bending, and a ball-and-socket joint that enables the palm to turn upwards and downwards.

SHOULDER This joint allows the arm to move in many directions.

HIP BONE Two hip bones and the sacrum link to form the pelvic girdle. The long bone of the leg (femur) forms a deep ball-and-socket joint with the hip bone. The knee is the intermediate joint of the lower limb, beautifully designed for stability and mobility. A long slender bone (fibula) lies alongside the smaller tibia, and together they form the top of the ankle joint.

HAND Because the hand has so many bones with moveable joints between them, it is capable of highly complex movements.

Inspired design
The skeleton is designed for stability, mobility, and protection.

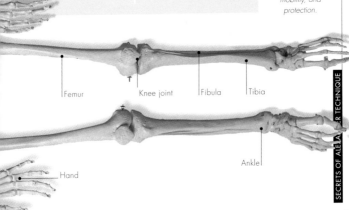

Femur

Knee joint

Fibula

Tibia

Ankle

Hand

The Art of Breathing

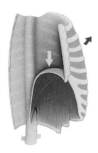

Inspiration
The diaphragm descends and flattens, elevating the lower ribs, expanding the lungs, and allowing breath to come in.

Exhalation
The diaphragm must relax to rise fully into a dome-like shape in readiness for the next time you breathe in.

The respiratory centre of the brain monitors the levels of oxygen and carbon dioxide in the lungs. When more breath is required, an impulse is sent to the diaphragm to contract, which causes it to flatten and descend. As it does so, it presses on the abdomen, which responds to the pressure by dropping and eventually resisting the downward movement. The abdomen then acts as a fixed point from which the diaphragm, assisted by the external intercostal muscles, elevates the lower ribs. The lungs, attached to the ribcage, are expanded by this movement as the chest is enlarged.

The breathing man
After exhalation and the subsequent expansion of the lungs by the movement of the diaphragm, atmospheric pressure now exceeds the pressure inside the lungs. That imbalance is quickly adjusted by an automatic reflex intake of air. Alexander found that retracting his head and over-contracting

throughout his body interfered with this reflex movement. He realized that restoring the free working of the primary control enabled effortless breathing. He was called "the breathing man" by his pupils because they experienced natural breathing as a result of his training.

When you breathe in, the action of the diaphragm on the viscera and abdominal muscles causes an increase of intra-abdominal pressure. During exhalation, this natural build-up of pressure, together with other elastic forces such as the muscles of the chest wall, the air pressure inside the lungs, and the torque of the ribs, causes the breath to leave the body naturally, independent of any muscular contraction. Although it is possible to consciously control breathing, it is useful for students of voice and those interested in a return to effortless breathing to experience the ease and power of this involuntary breathing cycle. Very often, an improvement in mood and a sense of wellbeing result from a return to natural breathing.

TWO-WAY STRETCH

When the head pivots forwards, the transference of weight allows the whole spine to lengthen. Gravity draws the feet, legs, and pelvis in the opposite direction. This lengthening up and down in opposite directions creates the antagonistic pulls in the body. Provided that the wish to lengthen and not collapse persists, this two-way stretch action will continue. When gravity is used effectively, the entire muscular system (at its full length) allows for the most efficient working of the body, and follows the natural rules of dynamic design.

Suspended support

It is important to stretch in all directions in order to achieve maximum support.

Miraculous balance
Exact equal and opposing force creates a self-supporting structure. This applies to the body framework as much as the structure of a building.

When you've got it, flaunt it!
Freedom and energy working together to achieve dynamic movement.

Extending Your Field of Awareness

Balance
You often interfere with the balance of the head on the neck, particularly during the fight or flight response.

The Alexander Technique helps you learn to be aware of the decisions you make in order to choose one course of action over another. As you progress through your lessons and apply yourself thoughtfully to the procedures in this book, you will become more aware of how you use yourself during all sorts of different activities. This knowledge can become a way of life and of knowing yourself better. Stopping, awareness of space, understanding the tensions required to deal with standing and moving, recognizing ingrained patterns of behaviour, considering the head–neck–back relationship, breathing awareness, making clear choices and electing how to carry them out – the Alexander Technique gives you a framework for understanding yourself.

Looking out, looking in

Training in the Alexander Technique helps you to extend your field of awareness. For this reason, you are encouraged to keep your eyes open when lying down. Often, your attention to the outside world causes you to lose awareness of yourself. Equally, you may shut your eyes to close out the world in order to relax and re-establish contact with yourself. There is often a connection between what is happening within you and the events in the outside world, such as a chance event, a changing relationship, or the way people respond to you.

Power of prevention

You probably tend to focus your attention on what you want and what you have to do to achieve your aims. The Alexander Technique encourages you to work out what you need to *prevent* to make this possible.

Instead of directing your awareness towards standing correctly, you are asked to be aware of the extent to which you interfere with the natural functioning of your balance and posture, and understand that if you can prevent unhelpful tensions occurring, a good stance can more easily result.

From here, you can consider your responses and personal goals. Imagine what it would be like if you were able to prevent boredom, anger, and frustration. Would happiness, grace, and a joy in being alive follow on naturally if your preventive sense was powerful enough to avoid unnecessary emotional intrusions? It is a fascinating prospect, and something to aspire to.

ALERT STILLNESS

The inhibitory signals ensure that you do not act until the appropriate moment and, when movement does occur, that the correct amount of energy is used and channelled efficiently. In this state of alert stillness, you have an integrated field of attention in which both the environment and the self are registered simultaneously. You may feel that stillness involves an effort, an over-preparation, or a collapse in which you lose energy and even fall into a trance. The Alexander teacher will help you to rediscover your alert stillness, and teach you how to stop and be quiet, yet stay awake. You will discover a stillness that contains inherent readiness for action.

Coordinated energy
Effective performance happens when ease, release, and effort work together in perfect harmony.

Balanced organisms

Ready for action: before each stroke, the rowers are powerful storehouses of energy that is waiting to be released into directed movement.

Readiness is all

You are designed for stillness that contains inherent readiness for action.

QUESTIONS & ANSWERS
A number of questions are frequently asked about the Alexander Technique, most of which require simple clarification of Alexander's own terminology. The most common queries are answered here to summarize the preceding chapters.

Q What is the primary control?

A *This refers to the head–neck–back relationship. Specifically, it is the neuromuscular mechanism that allows the neck to release in such a way that the head can go forwards and up, so that the spine can lengthen and the back can widen, in order to allow efficient breathing. Alexander realized that this primary relationship governed the freedom, efficiency and co-ordination of his movement. The discovery that the proper functioning of the primary control can be brought under conscious control through the application of inhibition and direction, is one of the enormous benefits of having lessons in the Alexander Technique.*

Q What is conscious inhibition?

A *Inhibition is the decision not to respond to a stimulus. Alexander knew from his own experience that if he could pause, stall his initial desire to speak, and instead give directions for the free working of the primary control, he could overcome his pattern of habitual misuse.*

Q What are directions?

A These are the instructions consciously given to the self to encourage correct use of the body. The directions are to let the neck be free so that the head can go forwards and up the spine can lengthen and the back widen. Together with conscious inhibition, these precise commands encourage the optimum functioning of the primary control.

Q What are proprioception and sensory appreciation?

A Proprioception is the unconscious process of determining position in space and the effort required to stay there. Sensory appreciation is the ability to judge that information. Faulty sensory appreciation refers to Alexander's observation that he could not feel the inappropriate muscular tension that was causing him to lose his voice.

Q What is a habit?

A A settled, often fixed, way of doing something without any conscious thought.

Q What is end-gaining?

A End-gaining is the tendency to focus on an end result while disregarding the process that you use to achieve that end. The tendency to misuse the primary control is related to this habit of moving quickly and thoughtlessly in order to reach a desired result.

Q What is "the means-whereby"?

A "The means-whereby" is a term used by Alexander to describe the art of paying attention to the process you use to achieve an end. The steps required to achieve a result become important. In order to overcome habitual misuse and improve the functioning of the primary control, greater sensitivity to the means-whereby is required – a conscious awareness of how much tension is used to achieve results.

TEACHERS IN ACTION

In an Alexander lesson you experience lightness, ease, and freedom in movement, and a general sense of wellbeing. Once you have started lessons, there is much you can do outside lesson time to help yourself. Your teacher will encourage you to observe how you use your mind to approach any activity. You may discover that you try too hard to get results, and that this is at the root of your postural and movement problems. ✍ The following procedures encourage you to deepen your experience of how the mind and body work together and, through thoughtful consideration, overcome your habits and help yourself.

Learning the Alexander Technique

Life is learning
Alexander always referred to himself as a learner, not a teacher. All of life is learning.

In order to learn the Alexander Technique, you must have lessons with a qualified teacher. Alexander teachers train for three years, over which time they learn awareness of balance, posture, and the nature of human reaction. The use of their hands is refined to develop a quality of touch that communicates the subtle messages of lightness and ease necessary to guide their pupils into balance. As teachers, they join the professional Society of Teachers of the Alexander Technique (STAT), which monitors standards and ethical codes of conduct.

How many lessons do I need?

Although profound changes in awareness can happen in one lesson, the subtle changes required need to be reinforced over time. A minimum of 20 lessons is suggested. It is one thing to get a new experience of your body in balance, but if, once you leave the lesson, you return to old patterns that are familiar, it should not be a surprise. The part of the brain that controls posture is unconscious and it takes time to establish new programs of response.

What happens in a lesson?

In an Alexander lesson, guided moving from sitting to standing is practised. Because sitting is performed regularly throughout the day, it is an ideal activity to use to develop the powers of inhibition and direction that will enable you to manage the task more efficiently. To sit still, freely and in balance, without slumping or tightening, requires a high degree of muscular awareness and control. When you sit in a chair, many of your habits are highlighted. Moving from sitting to standing is a stimulus that triggers your general tendency to over-react and try too hard – even the intention to move is sufficient to activate an over-tightening in your body. Chairwork forms the basis for a way of working which you can then apply to all movements during your day.

The semi-supine procedure is also practised. This technique involves lying down on a table with the head supported and the legs up. By changing your relationship to gravity, and by having the weight of your body supported entirely by the table, you are in an ideal situation to release muscular tension gradually.

Helping hands

During their training, Alexander Technique teachers learn to communicate balance, ease, freedom, and energy.

MEETING YOUR TEACHER

Alexander found that, although he could give a verbal instruction to his pupils, it was open to misinterpretation by them, so he began to guide his pupils gently with his hands. Alexander teachers continue to do this today, giving people a new experience of lightness and ease in everyday movement. By observing a pupil engaged in the mundane activity of sitting, the teacher gets a good idea of what needs to be addressed.

Considering the choices

By observing a pupil in the process of going from standing to sitting, an Alexander teacher is able to assess quickly the areas that need to be addressed.

Head forwards
and up

Gentle guiding
hand

Knees free to
go forwards

Learning to sit
*With the controlled yet gentle
use of his hands, the Alexander
teacher uses soft manipulation
to prevent any tension in the
pupil which is interfering with
freedom of movement.*

Learning How to Learn with the Technique

How to sit
Sitting, and moving in and out of a chair, tends to involve inappropriate muscular tension.

The Alexander Technique helps you appreciate the extent to which your impulses are working either for or against you. You may know what you want to do, but if you go too quickly for a result, your lack of conscious awareness of how you are performing and your impatience will spoil the outcome and exhaust you. This will frustrate you and provoke the opposite pattern of trying too hard, which will leave you drained of energy. These internal conflicts are universal – all human beings experience patterns that block both them and their potential.

Inherited tendencies

The fight or flight response, which evolved during our early history, continues to be a determining factor in how humans approach activity. The desire to get things right and the fear of getting things wrong may be based in those early instincts. Instinctive responses generate a tremendous amount of muscular energy, which is vital for getting you out of danger when you are in trouble. Inappropriate muscular effort may be an inability to manage those powerful energy potentials in contemporary situations.

The fight or flight response starts to be generated in everyday situations that are not life-threatening. It manifests physically as a fear reflex – the tightening of the neck muscles and a retraction of the head, the raising of the shoulders, and the holding of the breath. It is a panic response which we see every day as people try to cope with situations such as crossing the road. Alexander observed this pattern when he watched himself reciting in the mirror. He saw a movement in his body like the one made when frightened and that tension was interfering with the freedom required for speaking.

A new look at movement

Using sensory appreciation, inhibition, direction, the use of the primary control, and consideration of the means you use, helps you to gain the awareness to recognize when your instincts are working for or against you. It gives you a way to approach familiar activities so that clear intentions, strong determination, impulses, and energy work together towards an intended outcome.

HANDS

Alexander teachers are trained to use their hands in a very specific and disciplined way. Sometimes there is a sense of release felt not only in the response of your muscles, but in your whole self. You begin to feel that you can stop trying so hard and allow yourself to be guided by your teacher's hands. There is a feeling of safety and a recognition that these hands will not enforce change, but gently encourage you to go at your own pace. The other sensation you will experience is that the teacher is monitoring your tendency to try too hard by over-tensing your body.

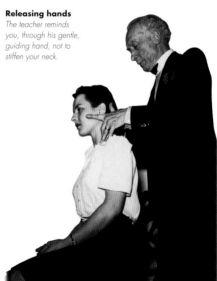

Releasing hands
The teacher reminds you, through his gentle, guiding hand, not to stiffen your neck.

Gentle strength
Alexander began teaching using verbal instruction, but found that, by using his hands to instruct pupils, his messages were much clearer.

Stand at your full height

The alert stillness of the teacher is communicated through their hands

Full stature

The teacher will encourage you to achieve your full height and remind you not to over-prepare for any action you might make.

Chair Work: Learning to Sit Comfortably

Guided sitting
The teacher will help you to sit comfortably at your full height without tensing your body.

How many times have you collapsed at the end of a busy day? The immediate feeling of relief soon goes and you begin to slump down in a heap. However, when sitting in a collapsed way, you could be putting up to 8 kilograms (18 pounds) of pressure on your joints and internal organs. You sat down to recover, but actually you are putting more strain on yourself. You have probably experienced this more acutely during a long journey, when you feel the need to get up at regular intervals to stretch your legs and back. Stiffness in the joints, indigestion, and swollen ankles are common results from sitting too long in a constricted way.

First considerations

The chair becomes a good stimulus for all your old habits to come into play. The way in which you begin to sit affects the end result quite dramatically. By taking the trouble to move from standing to sitting in a conscious, directed way, you are half-way to solving the problem of slumping. In Alexander Technique lessons, time is given to getting this procedure comfortably established so that you can prevent the problems that collapsing in a chair creates.

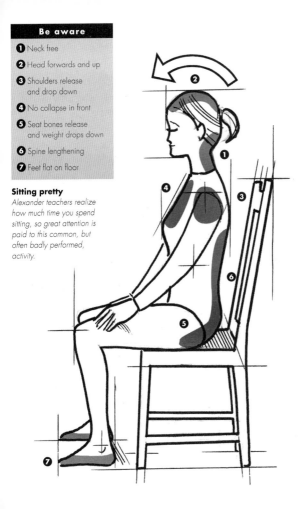

Be aware

1 Neck free

2 Head forwards and up

3 Shoulders release
and drop down

4 No collapse in front

5 Seat bones release
and weight drops down

6 Spine lengthening

7 Feet flat on floor

Sitting pretty

*Alexander teachers realize
how much time you spend
sitting, so great attention is
paid to this common, but
often badly performed,
activity.*

SITTING DOWN

It is important that you take a second to say "No" to the stimulus to sit. When you have done this, make the movement easily and lightly and when you feel the chair under you, straighten up and allow your weight to drop down through your sitting bones. Do not perch on the chair, but remember that your spine is lengthening in both directions – down as well as up. This creates the necessary tone in your back muscles to ensure that sitting straight is a painless process.

1 *Before you move, pause for a moment, and release your tendency to over-prepare for movement. Allow your neck to be free, your spine to lengthen and your back to widen.*

2 *Allow your eyes to drop as your head nods forwards slightly. Let your knees go forwards and your hips drop back in order to lower yourself in to the chair.*

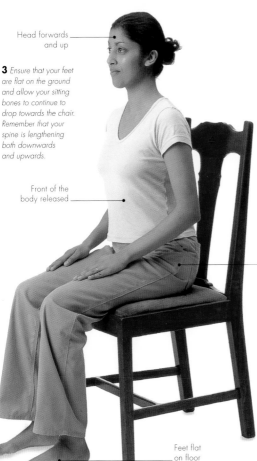

Head forwards
and up

3 *Ensure that your feet are flat on the ground and allow your sitting bones to continue to drop towards the chair. Remember that your spine is lengthening both downwards and upwards.*

Front of the
body released

Allow your
weight to drop
down through
your sitting bones

Feet flat
on floor

Reading without Strain

Reading lesson
Your teacher will remind you not to over-tighten your shoulders as you lift your book, and not to hold your breath.

We receive much of our information about the world from reading, and now the Internet furnishes us with volumes of information at the flick of a switch. Alexander Technique teachers know that the stimulus provided by the written word can be both a negative and positive one. Sometimes, we are not as efficient at reading as we would wish. When revising for examinations, we are often under pressure to read very quickly but at the same time understand the text fully and take in all the facts.

Performance problems

If you are a musician, you have to simultaneously read, comprehend, and play music without mistakes. No wonder you stiffen your neck, pull your head back, hold your breath, and generally panic. If you are required to read aloud, you have a recipe for disaster. Alexander found that it was in this very situation of reading, then reciting, that he first noticed how he misused himself and caused his own problems.

These reactions could come under the heading of psychological difficulties, but there are very real physical problems to be considered as well. The way you use your eyes is of primary importance. Your book or music needs to be positioned in such a way that you are not straining to see. An angled book is always preferable to having the book lying flat.

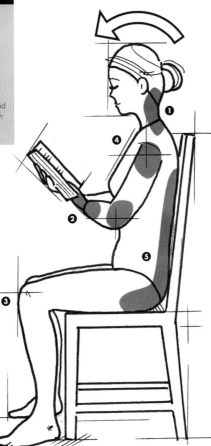

Be Aware

1 Neck and shoulders release to take weight of book

2 Free wrists, shoulders and elbows

3 Rest book on knees from time to time

4 Drop your shoulders and do not hold your breath

5 Release lower back

Sustaining focus

When you sit still for a long time you may tighten your body. It is worth taking a break from time to time to release your neck and change your focus.

READING WELL
Try to ensure that you keep your back lengthening and widening, and try not to narrow your upper chest as you lift your book up. By having the thought of letting your shoulders drop back and down you can help to keep them released. Naturally, when you lift the book, some muscles automatically begin to work. However, your aim is to be able to lift and hold the book with a minimum of effort. The distance from the text to your eyes is very important and keeping the book at an angle can help prevent strain of both neck and eyes.

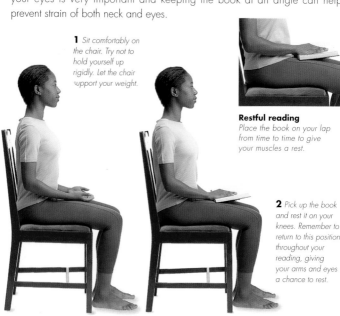

1 *Sit comfortably on the chair. Try not to hold yourself up rigidly. Let the chair support your weight.*

Restful reading
Place the book on your lap from time to time to give your muscles a rest.

2 *Pick up the book and rest it on your knees. Remember to return to this position throughout your reading, giving your arms and eyes a chance to rest.*

3 *Lift up the book by supporting the back of it with the other hand. Hold it at an angle of about 40° to your eyes.*

Try not to grab the book. Allow it to rest lightly in your hand, and use the other hand to hold it open.

The Art of Writing Easily

Extension
The movement of the pen on the page happens most efficiently when the fingers are free to flex and extend.

Flexion
Keep the arms, wrists, and fingers free and do not over-tighten the rest of your body while writing.

Now that so many of us are using keyboards rather than writing by hand, it may seem a little redundant to be concerned with the skill of forming legible letters. However, the act of writing has a deep-rooted connection to human evolution, as it involves the placing of the first finger and thumb together. This simple action, known as cortical opposition, is fundamentally important.

Humans developed the skill of being able to rotate the forefinger and thumb so that the sensitive pads could make direct contact with each other. This allowed for the precise holding of tools.

This stage marked a fundamental change in our evolutionary progress as people began to form more settled communities. They began to learn, rather than just survive. Simple pictorial writing was invented.

Communication

Children's first attempts at scrawling raise them to the level of written communicators. It is empowering to be able to define yourself in your own handwriting. It is amazing to consider how the messages from your head and your heart can, by writing, be simultaneously transcribed into words.

Be Aware

1. Neck free, head forwards and up
2. No collapse in front
3. Bend forwards from hips
4. Free wrist and hand
5. Use sloping surface

Free expression

If computers were suddenly no more you could still pick up a stick and write in the sand "the pen is mightier than the sword".

WRITING FREELY

By placing your thumb and forefinger together and flexing them, you create the necessary conditions in the hand and wrist that enable you to write easily. So often the fatigue and strain that you experience in your wrist are due to making too much effort when holding your pen. A sloping surface is helpful, because it gives support to your wrist and provides an appropriate angle for easy movement of the pen across the page. If the paper is at an angle to your eyes, you can expect to suffer less from straining of the neck and eyes. When you are helping children with writing, encourage them to take their time and allow the pen to do the work. When they start to dig holes in the paper, it is obvious that they are trying too hard.

1 *Remember not to hold your breath and try not to stiffen your elbows and wrists.*

2 *After coming forwards from your hips, gently pick up your pen. Hold it lightly between your thumb and forefinger. Your other hand can steady the paper.*

3 *Rest your hand lightly on the sloping surface. Try not to make any tension in your wrist or finger joint. Think about lengthening along your fingers.*

4 *Breathe out and gently flex your hand back from your wrist, so that your fingers are pointing up and your wrist remains free.*

6 *Take care not to grasp the pen. Allow it to rest between your forefinger and thumb. Do not press down.*

Your pen rests between your thumb and index finger

5 *Allow your thumb to rotate round so that it meets the pad of your index finger. Gently bend and straighten your thumb and fingers.*

Working Efficiently at the Keyboard

When you work at a keyboard, you tend to forget about your back and how you are sitting. Your eyes are continually occupied, looking at the screen and referring to the documents from which you are typing. When your eyes are constantly fixed on a point, or are moving from screen to document to keyboard, you tend to over-tighten your neck. The screen has a hypnotic effect and, if you aren't careful, you will start to go into a trance after a while and lose concentration.

Open your field of awareness
An expanded field of awareness will enable you to maintain a free and upright posture while you type.

Neck and upper back

When your hands are typing, there is a tendency to overwork the muscles of your neck and upper back. As you lean towards what you are doing, unless you consciously avoid it, you will tend to slump. Your body instinctively counteracts a collapse at the front by recruiting some muscles to tighten and hold you up. This usually causes people to end up with severe tension in the upper back region.

Regular breaks

Modern keyboards allow you to work at speed. However, the faster you work the more difficult it becomes to monitor what you are doing and the possibility of getting feedback from your body during the activity is diminished. From time to time, check to make sure that you have not been overtightening. Remember that regular breaks lead to increased productivity.

Be Aware

1. Shoulders released
2. Elbows at 90° to floor
3. Wrists free
4. Regular breathing
5. Wide upper back
6. Get up regularly

Remember yourself

Because your attention is drawn to the screen and what you are typing, you may forget about your posture.

TYPE FREELY

As soon as you sit in front of a computer, you immediately have the stimulus to pull down in front. Following the semi-supine position, you are more sensitive to this and can practise resting the hands on the keyboard and beginning to type slowly. This will enable you to maintain your direction in the vertical and begin the typing action easily, using only the muscles required. Fast typing may cause over-tightening in your hands, neck, back, and upper chest. Stop occasionally and check that your intention to release into the space above you equals your interest in what is in front of you.

1 *Before you start to type, pause to remember your head–neck–back relationship, free your neck, and drop your shoulders. Feel the weight of your elbows and your hands releasing and spreading on the table.*

2 *Begin slowly so that you can type by keeping your wrist free. As you speed up, be aware of when you begin to tighten. From time to time, pause and repeat step one.*

3 *Remember not to drop in front. If you need to take a closer look at the screen, bend forwards from the hips.*

4 *As your typing begins to speed up, keep your hands, wrists, and fingers free. Remember to pause from time to time and release through your arms, wrists, and hands, recover your full height, free your neck, and drop your shoulders.*

Drop your shoulders

Keep your wrists free

Keeping Your Cool Behind the Wheel

Pedal power
*Be sensitive to the power that lies
behind the wheel and remember
that speed can kill.*

Driving involves a lot of different considerations – you have to concentrate on the road, other drivers, and the direction you need to take in order to reach your destination. You have to be able to co-ordinate the car's controls if your drive is to be smooth and safe. Finally, your attitude to driving has an effect on how you perform. A lot depends on whether you are comfortable with the freedom and power that the car gives. Anxiety will

cause you to freeze up and be tentative in the decisions you make. Aggressive types have no difficulty making quick decisions and enjoy the extra power the vehicle gives them. But with the power and freedom go the added frustrations of the inevitable obstacles on the road – pedestrians, bicyclists, slow drivers, and, worst of all, traffic.

Applied inhibition

This conflict between having the desire and resources to reach a destination quickly, but being confronted by extraneous obstacles that prevent this, may explain the frustration and rage that some people experience behind the wheel. When you are stuck in a traffic jam, your end-gaining tendency starts to take over and you get more and more stressed. This is a great moment to test your powers of inhibition. Try to stop, free your neck, breathe out, and see whether you can be happy just to sit there with your thoughts.

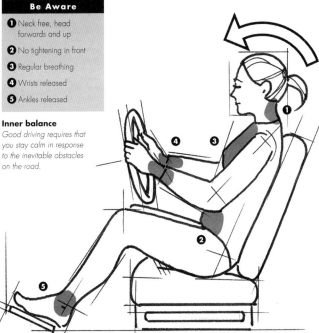

Be Aware

1. Neck free, head forwards and up
2. No tightening in front
3. Regular breathing
4. Wrists released
5. Ankles released

Inner balance

Good driving requires that you stay calm in response to the inevitable obstacles on the road.

CONSCIOUS DRIVING

Try to cultivate the attitude of patience. Remember that although it is important to get to your destination on time, if that means that you endanger yourself or others in the process, it is self-defeating. It is easy to forget that a car in the wrong hands becomes a lethal weapon. Take a moment before you get into your car to stop and stand still. Release your neck and rise up to your full height.

Collapsed

No alert stillness here. If you are in a collapsed position, you are paying insufficient attention to the road and are not ready to respond to an emergency.

Tightened

The stress of driving can cause you to tighten, hold your breath, and sit very badly.

Neck free,
eyes on
the road

Do not grip the
wheel tightly

Drop your
shoulders

Conscious

*Good drivers are the
ones who are able to
stay calm, deal with
emergencies, and
remain in control of
both themselves and
their vehicles.*

Let your foot
spread on
the ground

Restoring Balance

Lying down
*Constructive rest allows
your body to recover.*

Gravity exerts a constant downward pull on the body and even the most skilled movers use a certain amount of excessive effort to hold themselves up. Added to this, the pressure and pace of life compound the amount of muscular tension that builds up through the day, which in turn increases the difficulty of standing up.

Fear factor

The more we become unable to rely on the natural mechanisms of balance and posture, the more the fear of falling is exaggerated – and fear always means an increase in muscular tension. Fear speeds up our metabolism and accelerates our breathing rhythm, but underlying postural tensions resist the increasing metabolic rate. This means that further effort is required in order to satisfy our need for more breath, adding further disturbance to our natural posture. All deadlines, pressures, and anxieties compound the tensions in the body and collectively undermine what we take for granted – our ease and grace when standing up.

The semi-supine position

When we lie down in the semi-supine position, we are supported in such a way that we can release this burden. The whole of the back is supported and the unnecessary effort that we make to resist the downward pull of gravity can be released. The danger of falling down is removed and, along with it, the associated fear and anxiety. Confidence then emerges because, for the time being, the tension and effort associated with standing are not required.

The release of tensions that contract and contort the body permits it gradually to resume its shape, involving a subtle redirection, so that over time, the body begins to recover its true size. As your anxiety subsides and the body lengthens and widens, you stop holding your breath and the equilibrium of the natural breathing cycle – breathing out to breathe in – is restored. Allow your breath to go out and in through your nose. This filters, warms, and moistens the air on its way to your lungs. This is the most effortless way to breathe in helping you to prevent panic.

Time Well Spent

The benefit of lying down for a period each day allows the de-rotation and elongation of the spine to occur.

CONSTRUCTIVE REST

When you practise the semi-supine position, the head must be supported at the correct height. Use a rolled towel or T-shirt, or a pile of books. There is a natural curve to the spine, and having your head raised off the ground allows for this fact. When your head is properly supported, your neck releases in a way that promotes lengthening, widening, and free breathing. As you lie semi-supine, you are in an ideal situation to keep your mouth shut and breathe through your nose, which is calming. See pages 102–103 and 106–107 for more information.

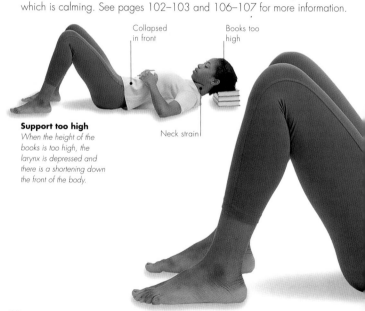

Collapsed in front

Books too high

Neck strain

Support too high
When the height of the books is too high, the larynx is depressed and there is a shortening down the front of the body.

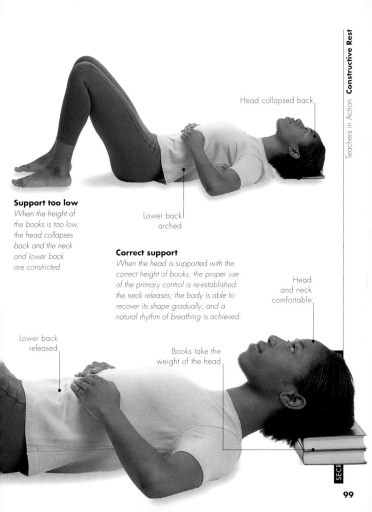

Head collapsed back

Support too low
*When the height of
the books is too low,
the head collapses
back and the neck
and lower back
are constricted.*

Lower back
arched

Correct support
*When the head is supported with the
correct height of books, the proper use
of the primary control is re-established:
the neck releases; the body is able to
recover its shape gradually; and a
natural rhythm of breathing is achieved.*

Head
and neck
comfortable

Lower back
released

Books take the
weight of the head

The Nine Points of Support

Release the neck
*The teacher's hands allow your
head to lengthen out and your back
to release on to the table.*

Lying down in the semi-supine position
gives you a chance to stop and
release tensions that have built
up during the day. The head weighs
between 4.5–6.8 kilograms
(10–15 pounds), and you carry this
around through every waking hour. By
lying down, you also take the weight

off your feet. The heavier parts of the
skeleton, which readily respond to
gravity and contact the ground, are
described as "weight-bearing".

Points of support

There are nine weight-bearing areas
when you are in the semi-supine
position: the back of the head, the right
and left side of the pelvis, the right and
left side of the upper back, the two feet,
and the two elbows. These points
provide a secure framework, allowing
you to recognize that you cannot fall
down, so you can stop trying to hold
yourself up. The process of release and
lengthening can then happen
spontaneously, provided that you stay
calm and patient. You may realize
that you are trying to speed

⑤

up the process of release. If this happens, remind yourself to stop and give yourself time, remembering the support of the nine weight-bearing areas of the back. The process of coming back into balance is deeply rooted, but it can be blocked if you are trying too hard to get results. Your aim is not actually to "do" something, but simply to stop interfering with the natural process of release.

Be Aware

1 Weight dropping down through back of head

2 Both shoulders

3 Both elbows

4 Both hips

5 Both feet

Spontaneous recovery

Release happens in its own good time. Be still, recover, and let gravity do the work.

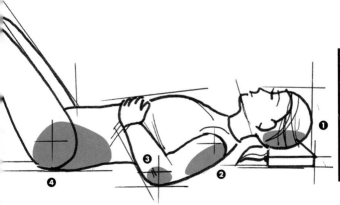

LYING DOWN

In order to prevent tightening or slumping, allow your neck to be free and your back to lengthen and widen. Shift your weight over one leg, remembering to lead with your head and to lengthen into the movement, not to over-contract and shorten. Lower yourself on to your knees. Then sit back on your heels, then on your buttocks. Roll gently backwards without stiffening your neck. As you lie on the ground and your body recovers its full size, you may be aware that you have been gasping air in through your mouth. It is more healthy to breathe through your nose.

1 Before you lower yourself to the ground or prepare to get up, apply the process of inhibition and direction. Lower yourself on to one knee.

2 Bring the other knee down and lower yourself on to your heels. When raising or lowering yourself, always remember to lead with the head.

Stop and release before movement

3 Sit on the ground with your arms wrapped loosely around your knees. Remember that you must not hold your breath. Then place your arms slightly behind you to take your weight and roll down on to the ground until your head is in contact with the books. See pages 106–107 for more information.

Allowing Your Body to Lengthen and Widen

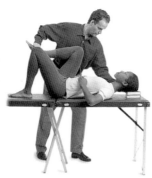

Releasing your joints
The teacher will help you release your knees and lower your leg to the table.

To assist the process of release, think about the nine weight-bearing points and how they support you, which allows your body the necessary time to change shape and become longer and wider. Your directions encourage these natural processes to take place. You have to think in such a way that you allow the action to take place in the body without

setting up more muscular tension. The Alexander Technique is based on the fact that before the right thing can happen, we have to prevent the wrong thing from taking place. Lengthening and widening rely on your preventive awareness. You have to stop the contractions that cause you to shorten and narrow. Lying in the semi-supine position allows you to stop shortening, narrowing, and contracting in a way conducive to finding your true size.

The elastic test

Hold a piece of elastic and draw the ends in opposite directions, and notice how the length increases and the elastic becomes springy. When the body

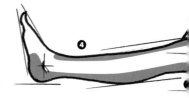

lengthens, it releases in opposite directions. For example, when you put your leg down, provided that you do not interfere with the process through too much effort, the sole of the foot eases away from the lower back and the distance between them increases. When you lift your leg up, you should notice that the pelvis has lengthened away from the back of the head and that the distance between your knees and pelvis has also increased.

Be Aware

1 Weight dropping through back of head

2 Don't brace hips, knees, or ankles

3 Allow back to lengthen

4 Allow leg to lengthen

5 Knee up

Long limbs

When you lower your leg muscles in your lower leg and back release so that lengthening in your leg can happen.

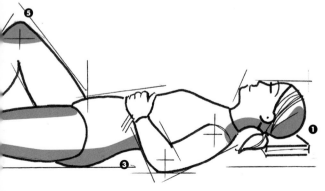

RELEASING YOUR LEGS

Because of the way in which the leg connects to the torso, there is an intimate relationship between any tightness in the legs or hips, and tension in the lower back and abdomen. When the leg is lowered to the ground, the muscles of the leg, hip, lower back, and abdomen gradually release. Thinking about sending the heel away from the lower back encourages the lengthening of the leg. This has a beneficial impact on your breathing. As the lower back and abdomen release, the external muscular tension that is limiting the action of the diaphragm is removed, and it becomes possible for this inner muscle to work more easily.

Flex the foot

1 When you lower one leg, this helps the lower back and abdomen to release. Keep thinking of releasing your other knee towards the ceiling.

Lengthening the legs encourages free breathing

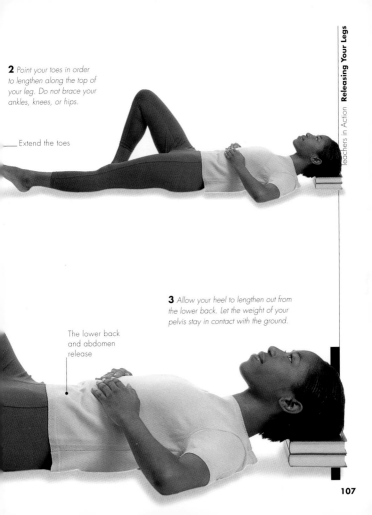

2 Point your toes in order to lengthen along the top of your leg. Do not brace your ankles, knees, or hips.

Extend the toes

3 Allow your heel to lengthen out from the lower back. Let the weight of your pelvis stay in contact with the ground.

The lower back and abdomen release

Widening Through Your Back

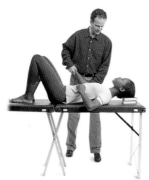

Widening
The teacher will help you release through your shoulders by gently moving your arm to the side.

The position and stability of the shoulder and upper chest area depend on muscles rather than joints. The fact that there are no fixed joints enables greater flexibility. A complex web of muscle allows the shoulders and arms to be lifted up, pulled down, drawn forwards towards the front of the body, or pulled back. If the muscles that move the shoulders are habitually tightened, or if one set of muscles is overworking, the upper chest loses its natural openness and width. Habitual tension, which causes the chest to narrow in this way, not only limits freedom of movement but affects the efficiency of the breathing mechanism.

Opening up

Lying semi-supine allows the muscles of your neck and upper back to release so that your natural width can be re-established. You cannot try to widen the back yourself, but you can take the necessary time to permit the release of the tensions that are causing the problem of narrowing. Taking the arms out to the side can be helpful, as it makes you aware of any body tension. This position encourages you to understand that the muscles in the body can pull the shoulders in many different directions at the same time: up, in, back, and down. This can result in a permanent state of tension in the shoulders. Over time, the tightening that is pulling the shoulders up and in will release, allowing them to drop down. At the same time, the muscles that pull the shoulders down will release and they are then free to ease up from below.

Be Aware

❶ Weight of head on support

❷ Shoulders, elbows, wrists released

❸ Upper chest widened

❹ Back lengthened and widened

Open-hearted

By taking the time to allow the release of the tensions that are causing narrowing, widening through the upper chest can be re-established.

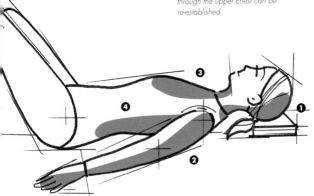

PREVENTIVE AWARENESS

It is important to pay attention to the feedback you are getting from your body so you become aware of when you start to try too hard and end-gain. If you go directly for a result, it will only lead to further tension, which interferes with widening. If at any point you start to tighten the neck, stiffen the shoulders, lock the elbows or wrists, or hold your breath, stop and once again allow the release to happen.

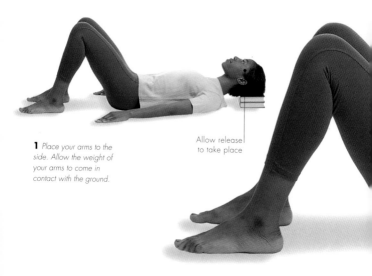

1 *Place your arms to the side. Allow the weight of your arms to come in contact with the ground.*

Allow release to take place

2 *Place one arm out to your side.
Release your neck, upper back,
shoulders, elbows, and wrists. Bring
your hand back on to your lower ribs
and then take your other arm to the side.*

Free the
neck

Do not brace the
shoulders, elbows,
or wrists

3 *Think of sending your
fingers into the space beyond
them, in order to widen
through the upper chest.*

Widen thourgh
the upper chest
as you breathe

Free the wrists

Supporting Your Body on All Fours

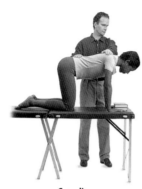

Crawling
The teacher allows the head to gently lead forwards, while the back remains flat and lengthened.

Crawling is one of the early stages of our development. As a child, learning to support the body on all fours develops the subtle strength and sense of balance that are required to stand up easily and move gracefully. This encourages the correct use of the postural muscles and awakens the supporting spine in such

a way that the child gains the confidence to stand up on two legs. This allows an increased field of vision and frees up the arms so that the learning of manual skills can begin.

Back to basics

The aim, when adopting the crawling position, is once again to explore the possibility of supporting your head and body with minimal muscular strength and to enable the spine to lengthen. This is a basic requirement for being able to stand in balance and move freely. When you lie in the semi-supine position, your head is supported in such a way that your neck is able to be a continuation of your spine. The spine lengthens and the front of the body becomes free and open. When you roll over into the crawling position, you may find that your head tends to droop. In order to prevent this, you may overuse the muscles of the neck, tighten the front and hold your breath. The crawling exercise helps to make you aware of which muscles you over-contract, interfering with your inherent ease and freedom of movement.

Subtle strength
We are designed to support ourselves on all fours with ease and grace.

Be Aware

❶ Do not tighten neck and upper back

❷ Allow head to nod forwards

❸ Hands under shoulders

❹ Knees under hips

❺ Back suspended

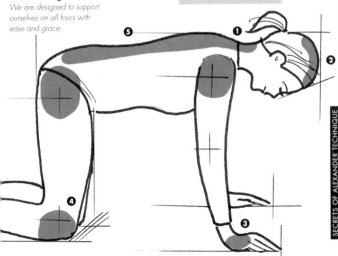

CRAWLING

When you adopt the crawling position, place your knees hip-width apart, and your hands shoulder-width apart. You do not want to be holding yourself up or sinking down. Keep your back long and flat and do not collapse down in the front part of your body. After a while the neck, upper back, front of the chest, biceps, and abdomen may begin to tighten. Return to semi-supine, supported through the nine weight-bearing points, and the areas that have become over-contracted will release.

1 Lying in the semi-supine position enables you to stop tightening your muscles unnecessarily.

2 Raise one arm above your body so that your fingers are pointing directly towards the ceiling and then look to one side.

Release your neck and shoulders to extend your arm

3 Let your eyes lead your head and your arm lead your body as you roll over on to your side, and then move into the crawling position

Release your neck as your eyes lead your head

4 With a limb at each corner, your body weight is evenly distributed through your legs and arms. It is important to let your weight settle easily between these four areas. When you are no longer able to maintain this position productively, roll back into the semi-supine position.

Spine lengthens

Everyday Movements

Squatting
Before chairs were invented, this was the natural way to sit. It is still common in some cultures.

basis of change and development through the Alexander Technique. It is a practical antidote to your tendency to over-react to stimuli. Perhaps you found it difficult to lie still and were frustrated that results were not being achieved quickly enough. This was an encounter with exactly the thoughts and impulses that cause you to work against yourself. It is these very habits of the mind that you are attempting to recognize and deal with through your ability to inhibit.

Clarity

During your work on constructive rest, you will start to notice fundamental postural and physiological changes. These changes allow a return to your natural shape, and are valuable for health. If you manage to lie down in the evening, it provides an excellent way of recovering at the end of a challenging day. It allows you to clear your mind of the clutter that has accumulated during the day and gives you the opportunity for some clear thinking.

B y practising constructive rest, you have begun to explore parts of yourself that are a primary part of your functioning as an upright human. Persistent repetition will enable you to use your mind and body more consciously to apply yourself to the activities of living. The first thing you will notice is the inhibitory process of pausing before an activity. This is the

Mind–body unity

To apply the Alexander Technique to your daily actions, you need to develop the skills of inhibition and direction. Everyday activities involve different types of movement. It is likely that you will over-react to the stimulus to perform the actions, and this will cause you to shorten and narrow the body and restrict your breathing. However, what is actually required throughout is the intention to stop and give yourself the time needed to recover your full stature before, during, and after each activity. The Alexander Technique encourages a mind–body initiative that enables you to face the demands of a busy life while remaining aware of any tendency to over-react and over-contract. In order to help yourself learn the principles and apply them to simple everyday tasks, get in touch with your local Alexander teachers. They help you to understand the connection between over-reaction and loss of full stature and help you to take charge of yourself. It is not what you do but the way that you do it.

DYNAMIC BENDING

Much of our day is spent bending. Many activities are no longer available to us if we lose this ability. Most of the injuries that are caused through bending happen as a result of a quick, ordinary movement – "I bent down in the garden to pull up some weeds", or "I had just lifted the box and could not straighten up again". The problem comes because we do not really consider how we bend. In the following sections we will consider the best means of achieving the optimum working order of bones, joints, and muscles. Remember that the procedures are opportunities to apply the processes of inhibition and direction and that success is not possible without them.

1 Let your head nod gently forwards as your ankles, knees, and hips release.

2 Continue to allow your knees to bend and the weight of your body to counterbalance the tendency to fall forwards.

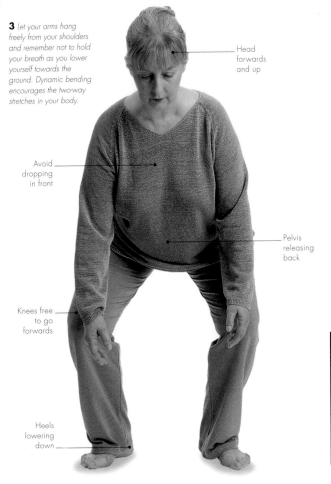

3 *Let your arms hang freely from your shoulders and remember not to hold your breath as you lower yourself towards the ground. Dynamic bending encourages the two-way stretches in your body.*

Head forwards and up

Avoid dropping in front

Pelvis releasing back

Knees free to go forwards

Heels lowering down

Learning How to Bend

Hands on back of chair
This procedure can encourage the two-way stretches in your body, leading to increased muscle tone.

I n an Alexander lesson, your teacher helps you understand what happens when you begin to move. In order for any movement to take place, your joints must be able to flex. Your ankles, knees, hips, and neck need to be free. Although these joints differ in structure, they fulfil the same requirement in providing a way for your bones to move. Without joints, you could not

move at all and your body would be rigid and immobile. Learning a different way of bending plays an important part in retraining your musculature.

Counterbalancing

Before you start to bend, place your feet a little further apart than when you are standing naturally. Inhibit your tendency to over-prepare and give your directions. Allow your head to nod gently forwards, and as this happens your spine will have a chance to lengthen in both directions, up and down. As your head moves forwards, it acts as a counterbalance to your body weight, which is moving backwards as your knees and ankles bend.

Bending needs to be considered and fluid, with your head nodding forwards, your back moving backwards and your knees moving forwards. Avoid collapsing in front and holding your breath. Your arms should hang freely by your sides. As you move forwards, your arms also move so you are ready for any work that needs to be done.

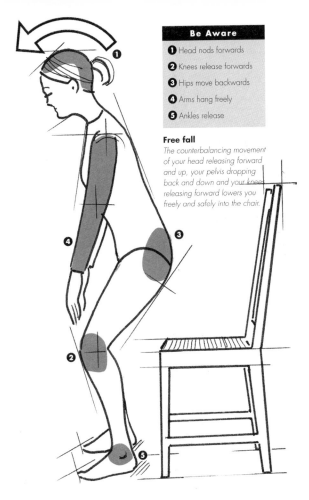

Be Aware

❶ Head nods forwards

❷ Knees release forwards

❸ Hips move backwards

❹ Arms hang freely

❺ Ankles release

Free fall

The counterbalancing movement of your head releasing forward and up, your pelvis dropping back and down and your knees releasing forward lowers you freely and safely into the chair.

HANDS ON CHAIR

This is a useful way of co-ordinating back muscles and free breathing with the performance of a very specific activity. Bend forwards and gently place your hands, palms up, on the back of a chair. Then turn your hands over and lightly grasp the back of the chair with your fingers and thumbs pointing directly down. Try to keep your wrists free and your forearms parallel to the ground as you hold the chair. When your upper limbs are free, you can begin to allow your back muscles to do most of the work. Your body weight can be used as a counterbalance so that you can establish a lengthening away from your hands – called "pulling to the elbows". This prevents your tendency to grasp the chair.

1 *Lower yourself into the bending position. Release your neck and allow your hands to hang by your side. Raise your arms, one by one, and place your hands, palm up, on the back of the chair. Drop the weight of your arms and open through the upper chest.*

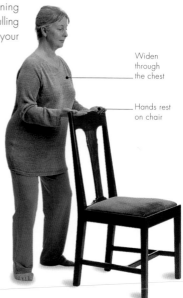

Widen through the chest

Hands rest on chair

2 *Turn your hands over and lightly grasp the back of the chair, with your fingers and thumbs pointing directly down. Keep your hands and wrists free. Think of dropping and drawing your elbows away from each other.*

The thumb and forefinger oppose each other without tightening the wrist

Neck, hips, knees, ankles, elbows, and wrists release

3 *Let your knees go forwards and your hips go back. This will activate the two-way stretch in your back and free your breathing.*

Opening Your Back

Self-support

The teacher will help you learn how to use your hands on a flat surface and counterbalance your weight.

Sensible bending

By considering how you bend, letting your head nod forwards, your hips move backwards, and your knees go forwards and away, you create good tone in your muscles. If you can develop the two-way stretch in your back and legs, you can maintain an energized posture with minimum stress on your joints. Your forearms can be used in a free and released way that keeps your back wide, so easy breathing is maintained.

Practise putting your hands on a flat surface and gently transferring your weight on to them so they become weight-bearing, then rock back on to your heels, and you will experience real freedom in the shoulders and upper chest. Your body moves forwards between your arms and your long postural back muscles are given the chance to stretch, both towards your head and back to your hips. The antagonistic pull of your muscles allows you to remain bending for a much longer time than you have probably experienced before.

Artists and architects use specially designed equipment for their work, but most of us have to work on surfaces that are too low to be used in a fully upright posture, and so we have to bend. Inevitably, the collapsed posture we adopt starts to cause problems.

Be Aware

1. Head forwards and up
2. Shoulders released
3. Weight forwards on hands
4. Chest widening
5. Hips released back and down
6. Ankles released

Weight transfer

Transferring your body weight onto your hands helps you to practice not over-tightening in the neck and upper back.

SUPPORT YOUR WEIGHT

It is useful to take a moment to consider the way you bend over the ironing board, the workbench, the kitchen sink or the car engine. When you use your hands in any of these activities, you usually make too much effort and over-involve your neck and shoulder muscles. By practising the following procedure, you will give your upper limbs the experience of being weight-bearers. This will help to prevent too much work being done by the muscles of your shoulders and upper back. As you allow your weight to come forwards on to your hands, you will help keep your wrists free and stop some of the heavy, gripping movements you tend to make when working with your hands while bending over.

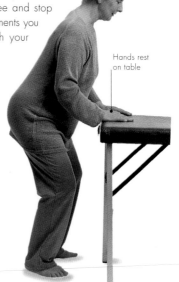

Hands rest on table

1 *Lower yourself into the bending position. Release your neck and place your hands on the surface in front of you. Drop the weight of your arms and open your chest.*

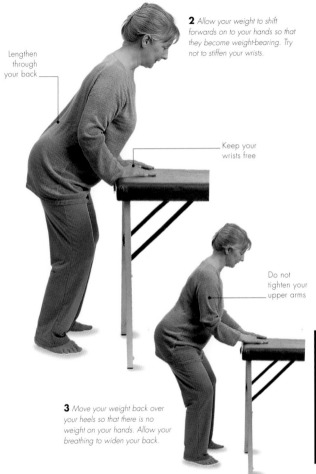

Lengthen
through
your back

2 *Allow your weight to shift forwards on to your hands so that they become weight-bearing. Try not to stiffen your wrists.*

Keep your
wrists free

Do not
tighten your
upper arms

3 *Move your weight back over your heels so that there is no weight on your hands. Allow your breathing to widen your back.*

The Benefits of Squatting

Sitting without a chair
With your teacher's help, this procedure becomes easier as your knees, hips, and ankles become more flexible.

Young children move from standing to squatting with no trouble at all. They see something they wish to pick up and in an instant they are down on the ground and up again walking off with the object. You could argue that they are so close to the ground that it is easy for them, but squatting is an important physical action that you should not lose.

Beneficial stretch

Being able to rest with your knees and ankles fully flexed gives both your long back muscles and your leg muscles a beneficial stretch. It also stimulates your internal organs and helps with elimination. Your Alexander Technique teacher will help you to rediscover this useful skill and take you slowly into the squat, going just as far as is comfortable for you and no further.

Time to release

At first it may seem that you will never be able to keep your heels flat on the floor and go all the way to the ground but, with help, you will slowly get a released stretch throughout your body that enables you to perform an easy squat. Remember that you need to keep releasing your neck and letting your head nod forwards so that the diagonal line of the head, neck, and back is maintained throughout the movement. Do not hold your breath or overestimate the difficulty of the movement and give up before you even try.

Be Aware

❶ Head forwards

❷ Hips back and down

❸ Heels on floor (if possible)

❹ Back lengthening

❺ Arms hanging freely
or used to support

Released stretch

*Squatting is a pleasurable
activity. It puts a stretch
throughout your body.*

SQUATTING

Follow the simple steps of letting your head go forwards, hips go backwards, and knees go forwards, and see how far you can go. If you really want to try and get down to the floor, hold on to something fixed, such as a banister, and counterbalance yourself against this reliable anchor. Do not repeat the exercise too many times, do not try to go further than you can, and remember that the end is just as important as the beginning. Returning to a standing position requires that you let your head go forwards and up, and you are careful not to hold your breath or help with your arms.

1 Stand with your feet slightly wider than your hips. Before you lower yourself to the ground, pause to allow your neck to be free so that your spine can lengthen.

2 Begin to lower yourself towards the ground by letting your head nod forwards, your pelvis drop down, and your knees release forwards.

Hips free to drop back

Neck free to allow head to nod forwards

Knees free to go forwards

3 *Continue to let your head go forwards and up, your pelvis back and down, and your knees forwards over your feet.*

4 *Release your neck and allow your head to nod forwards. Let your pelvis drop away from your head. In this position you put a natural stretch on the muscles throughout your body.*

Neck released

Feet flat on floor

Bending Effectively When Lifting and Carrying

Easy lifting
It is possible to lift without creating undue tension in your hands, wrists, and arms.

When you come to lift and carry something, you are faced with two separate problems: the weight of the object, and how to balance it while moving. In some cultures, women balance enormous weights on their heads and still move freely and effortlessly.

Using body weight

In the section on bending, you have learnt how to use the weight of your body as a counterbalance. When you have to lift something, you need to make sure that the distance you are going back is equal to the weight that you are trying to lift. Your tendency will be to come down in the front of your body, hold your breath, and over-stiffen your arms. None of these will help you any more than bracing your legs and gritting your teeth.

Leg work

Because the muscles in your thighs are very strong, they tend to do too much of the work. You should be using your back muscles and your actual body weight freely. Test the weight of the object to be lifted, so that you do not start to end-gain and over-prepare because you have wrongly estimated the weight and the effort needed. When you are faced with lifting a living being, another set of stimuli are evoked. These are often associated with fear, such as dropping the baby, hurting the kitten, or being bitten by the snake.

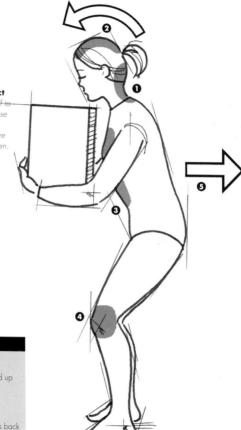

Think before you act

Before you lower yourself to pick something up, release your neck and give your directions to let your entire body musculature lengthen.

Be Aware

1 Neck free

2 Head forwards and up

3 Breathe out

4 Bend knees

5 Own weight moves back as a counterbalance

APPLIED INHIBITION

When you come to lift something, remember the importance of saying "No" before you begin. When you are presented with a stimulus that you feel unable to deal with, you must return to your directions. Perhaps the suitcase is too heavy or the pot too hot – your initial response will be to tighten and to hold your breath. You need to change this first of all. Then you can consider your directions and your breathing, and check that you have not over-prepared and made too much effort in your muscles, particularly those in your neck and shoulders, and hands. Take a moment to stretch your fingers towards the ground before you bend to pick up the object. When carrying heavy loads, take frequent breaks and remember to change the weight from side to side. A backpack is preferable to carrying weight on one side of your body.

1 Before you lift, pause for a moment and do not over-tighten in your neck, arms, shoulders, and legs. This will allow the counterbalancing movements in your body to happen.

Do not
stiffen your
arms

2 Be careful not to grip the
box too tightly or to hold your
breath, and use your weight
as a counterbalance as you
begin to lift.

Do not overestimate
the weight of the
object

3 By not stiffening your
arms and not holding your
breath, you will not
overestimate the weight
of the object and should
therefore find it easier
to lift than you expected.

The Cross-Pattern Reflex

Crawling position
Your teacher will help you to keep the antagonistic pulls in the long muscles of your back by allowing your head to go forwards and your hips to go back.

When babies make their first moves forwards, they begin by squirming along on their stomachs towards whatever draws their attention. Soon, they are able to bring their knees under the body, support themselves on their hands and start to move towards their desired target more quickly. In this position, they mirror the action of four-legged animals, following a pattern in which the head and spine are moving in the same horizontal plane.

Influence on development

When this happens, one of the basic reflexes, called the cross-pattern reflex, begins to develop. As the right knee moves forwards, so does the left hand, then this is repeated on the opposite diagonal. The left–right, right–left pattern has a fundamental effect on the development of co-ordination. Current research suggests that crawling also affects the attainment of the skills of comprehension, letter recognition, and reading. When a baby misses out this stage and is perhaps a "bottom bouncer", subsequent reading problems may occur. Babies spend hours practising crawling, and this should be encouraged. The desire to get them up on to two legs to start walking should not be forced on them before they are ready. This stage of development should be enjoyed and not hurried.

Be Aware

❶ Do not lift the head

❷ Do not tighten in front

❸ Lengthen along the back

❹ Put full weight on all four limbs

A fundamental pattern
Crawling is a beneficial action for co-ordination of movement.

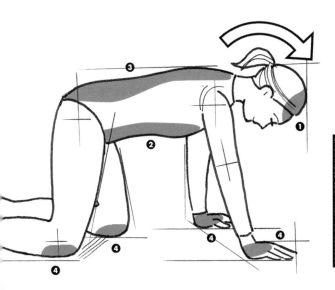

THE CRAWLING MOVEMENT

For babies, crawling is their natural way of moving forwards before they learn to walk. You can also benefit by returning to this basic procedure of being on all fours and moving forwards with your head leading your body. When you adopt the crawling position, you re-engage the use of your arms as forelegs. The movement from left to right and right to left establishes the cross-pattern reflex. A good, balanced rhythm in crawling helps your co-ordination. Be careful not to let your back sag down and try not to collapse in front.

1 *Release your neck and allow your head to turn gently to one side to look at your right hand.*

2 *Slide your right hand and your left knee forward. Allow your neck to be free so that your head can lead you into the movement.*

Allow your knee and hand to move together

Breathing out helps to thrust you forwards into the movement

3 The head leads and the body follows as you breathe out into the movement.

Release your neck to turn your head

4 Leading with the head, turn your eyes to the left as you slide your right knee and your left hand forwards.

The Star Procedure and the Two-Way Stretch

Star experience

As you experience the two-way stretch in your body, you will notice that your breathing becomes freer and more regular.

When the abdomen and chest muscles flex, it is equivalent to having an 8-kilogram (18-pound) weight hanging from your neck. Because these muscles are so strong, the muscles in your back have to tighten to counteract the downward pull in the front of your body

and stop you falling forwards. If your body is over-contracted, you will also apply too much effort when you try to lift your arms. This makes it difficult to achieve your full reach. Therefore the amount of energy expended, with the muscles of the front and back of your body working against each other, makes standing up a tiring activity and the weight of your arms, as they are raised above your head, soon becomes unbearably heavy.

Diagonal directives

The Star procedure can lead to a greater appreciation of the diagonal movements in your body that facilitate a two-way stretch, helping you to stand at your full height with less effort and to extend your limbs. When you raise your arms, you may become aware that you are tightening your neck, chest, and abdominal muscles. The process of inhibition helps you to stop and recognize it. As you release the unnecessary effort

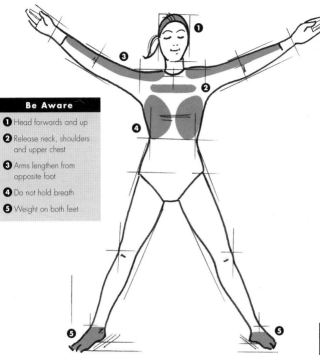

Be Aware

❶ Head forwards and up

❷ Release neck, shoulders and upper chest

❸ Arms lengthen from opposite foot

❹ Do not hold breath

❺ Weight on both feet

that you are making in the front of your body, less effort in the muscles of your back is required. You will then be able to increase the two-way stretch movement by directing your fingers into the space beyond your reach.

Release into action

As you raise your arms and send your hands and feet away from each other, try to avoid tightening your neck and upper back.

THE STAR PROCEDURE

Stand with your feet slightly wider than your hips. Let your arms hang freely at your sides and check that their weight is not causing you to narrow through your chest. Raise your arms, individually and then both together, by reaching into the space beyond your fingers and stop at the point where the arms are extending out from the back at a 45° angle. Think about your hands going away from your upper back, and your legs going towards the ground, which together facilitate the two-way muscle stretch through your body.

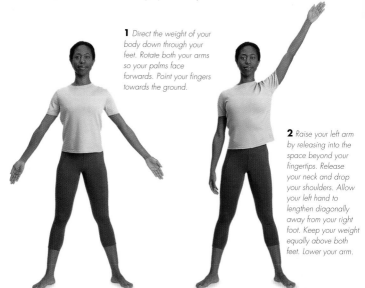

1 Direct the weight of your body down through your feet. Rotate both your arms so your palms face forwards. Point your fingers towards the ground.

2 Raise your left arm by releasing into the space beyond your fingertips. Release your neck and drop your shoulders. Allow your left hand to lengthen diagonally away from your right foot. Keep your weight equally above both feet. Lower your arm.

Teachers in Action **The Star Procedure**

3 Raise your right arm by releasing into the space beyond your fingers. Drop your shoulders and allow your right hand to lengthen diagonally away from your left foot. Lower your arm.

4 As you direct your fingers into the space beyond your reach, widen through your chest as you raise both your arms.

To facilitate the muscle stretch in your body, your hands release out from your upper back and your legs release towards the ground

5 Continue to raise your arms to the point where they are extending out from the back at a 45° angle. Think of your hands releasing out from your upper back and your legs going towards the ground. Lower your arms by releasing into the space beyond the fingertips.

SECRETS OF ALEXANDER TECHNIQUE

Free Your Breathing

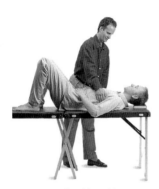

Unrestricted breathing
Your teacher will help you pay attention to your breathing and allow the natural release to happen.

The ability to be heard and to communicate is one of our most basic survival responses. For example, babies use their voices to alert their mothers to their need for food, warmth, love, and attention. In order to create sound, you need breath. Any voice work should consider whether your posture and breathing are enabling you to make sounds both freely and energetically.

Posture and breathing

To make sounds, your body needs to be lengthening and widening so that your ribcage is free to swing down and in towards your centre of gravity. Posture requires stability and breathing requires movement. The Alexander Technique helps these two seemingly opposite requirements to work together in harmony, giving you the experience of full sound resonating in your body, empowering you to make sound, be heard, and interact with the world around you.

The out-breath

After years of being told to "take a deep breath", you may have got used to concentrating on your in-breath. When you focus on breathing out, and then simply allow the intake of breath to happen, significant changes occur. When you were born, you cleared your lungs by an outward action. The subsequent intake of breath was an automatic response to that movement. Breathing can be rhythmic and natural, but we often tend to hold our breath in response to stress. This sets up a habit pattern where the ribs are tight and it is a struggle to breathe in.

Be Aware

1. Neck free, spine lengthened
2. Release the front of your body
3. Hands on lower ribs
4. Do not hold the breath
5. No tension in mouth, jaw, or face

Breathe out to breathe in

Lengthening and widening as you breathe out will lead to an effortless in-breath.

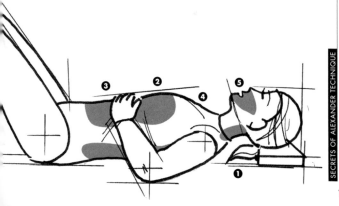

POSTURE AND BREATHING

When you lie in the semi-supine position, the body has a chance to release, and a lengthening and widening can occur. This allows your ribcage to free up and the natural movement of breathing is restored. Shape your mouth as if to blow out a candle and relax the breath out through the lips with an "fff" sound. Close your mouth and let the breath return through your nose. Repeat the cycle three times. During the exercise your upper chest may have collapsed as your ribs swung down and in. Perhaps you stiffened your neck and braced your body in order to prevent it from collapsing. When you pause and rest, you can begin to recognize these patterns. Release and re-establish your full height and width.

1 *Breathe out with an "fff" sound. Allow your neck to be free and your spine to lengthen. Widen through your upper chest as you let your ribs swing down and in. Don't interfere with the movement of the ribs. Close your mouth and let yourself breathe in through your nose.*

Widen upper chest to breathe out

Allow ribs to move down and in

2 *Avoid interfering with the movement of the ribs so that the full energy of the out-breath becomes available. If you allow yourself to breathe out, breathing in can happen automatically. Repeat the cycle three times and then rest. Did you brace or collapse during the exercise?*

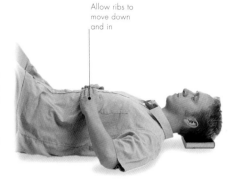

3 *Hum a note that is in the middle of your range. A free neck, a lengthening spine, and a wide upper chest help you to keep your throat open and toned so your sound can vibrate in your body.*

Feel your sound vibrating

Vocal Preparation

The Whispered "Ah"
The teacher will help you practise this prior to any voice work you may need to do – it is an excellent preparation.

order to stretch the vocal folds and create enough space on the inside of your body for your voice to sound loudly and clearly. The procedure known as the "Whispered 'Ah'" helps all these activities to work together.

Before you whisper the "ah" sound, pause for a moment to make sure that your neck is free and your head is able to go forwards and up so that your spine can lengthen and your back can widen. Tensions in the body close the throat and restrict breathing. When you lengthen and widen, you release your ribcage and throat – both essential requirements for a good working voice.

Say "ah"

Allow the tip of your tongue to rest against the back of your lower teeth and think of something that makes you smile. These thoughts increase the release and opening of the throat and relax the face so that your jaw can open freely. Then whisper "ah" in a loud, open, sustained way. As soon as you finish the sound, close your mouth and breathe in through your nose.

Your body and voice are deeply connected. One of the first indications that you are not well is a change in the strength of your voice. Equally, for your voice to work most effectively, your body must be freely balanced, with good breath support available to activate the movement of the vocal folds. Your throat needs to be unconstricted and open in

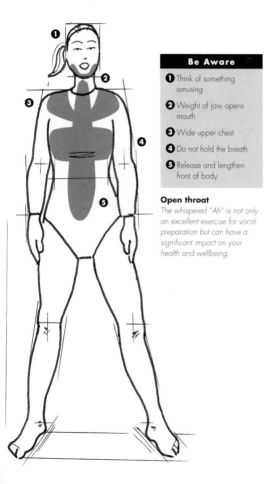

Be Aware

1. Think of something amusing
2. Weight of jaw opens mouth
3. Wide upper chest
4. Do not hold the breath
5. Release and lengthen front of body

Open throat

The whispered "Ah" is not only an excellent exercise for vocal preparation but can have a significant impact on your health and wellbeing.

THE WHISPERED "AH"

When Alexander freed his neck so that his head went forwards, his spine lengthened, and his back widened, he created the conditions necessary for his voice to work well. Freeing the ribcage, stretching the vocal folds and opening the resonant spaces in the chest, throat, mouth, and head happens when the body is at its full height. The Whispered "Ah" is an excellent exercise for applying the principles of the Technique and overcoming the habits that interfere with your vocal potential. It will also help to improve your health and sense of wellbeing.

1 *Breathe out with an "fff" sound. Allow your neck to be free and your spine to lengthen. Widen through your upper chest as you allow your ribs to swing down and in. Don't interfere with the movement of the ribs. Close your mouth and let yourself breathe in through your nose.*

2 *Think of something that makes you smile. This helps to open the facial resonators, release your throat, and activate your breathing.*

3 _Allow the tip of your tongue to rest against the back of your lower teeth. Think of something amusing and say "ah" in a loud, open, sustained whisper. Remember to close your mouth and breathe in through your nose._

Support Your Voice

Antagonistic pulls
The teacher helps you maintain the antagonistic pulls throughout your body as you lengthen into a released sound.

When you want your voice to be heard in a large space or over a long distance the amount of breath you require increases. Automatically more effort will be made in your abdominal muscles to support your voice. The abdominal muscles are extremely strong and are capable of bracing your ribcage and pulling your body down. If this happens then your throat will be constricted and your vocal folds will lose their stretch. This can lead to irritation and eventual damage if misuse of your voice continues. A vicious circle is set up whereby fixing the ribcage means that you will then have to fight for your next breath. Struggling to breathe in makes it likely that the next vocalization will require inappropriate effort. As a result, your voice will start to sound strained and lose much of its quality.

Using the Star procedure

Efficient posture ensures that the supporting muscles of the voice function with the right degree of effort. The Star procedure helps you focus on your posture, maintaining the antagonistic pulls through your body by lengthening and widening. It ensures appropriate activity in your supporting muscles. When you practise sounds be aware of when you are no longer comfortable reaching into the space beyond your fingers. This signifies that you have slumped or over-contracted your body. At this point you need to lower your arms, apply your directions, and then assume the Star position once again.

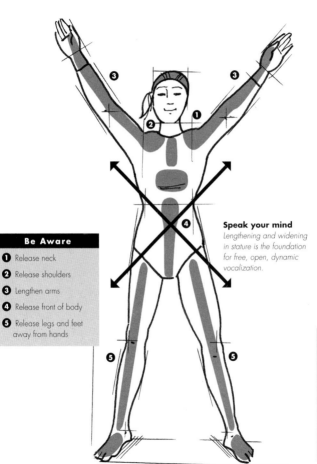

Be Aware

1. Release neck
2. Release shoulders
3. Lengthen arms
4. Release front of body
5. Release legs and feet away from hands

Speak your mind
Lengthening and widening in stature is the foundation for free, open, dynamic vocalization.

BREATHING AND VOICE

Allow your neck to be free, so that your head can go forwards and up, your spine can lengthen, and your back can widen. Raise your arms into the star position. Direct your fingers into the space beyond them and breathe out with an "fff" sound. Close your mouth and allow the air to return through your nose. Say "ah" in a whisper three times, each time closing the mouth and allowing the air back in.

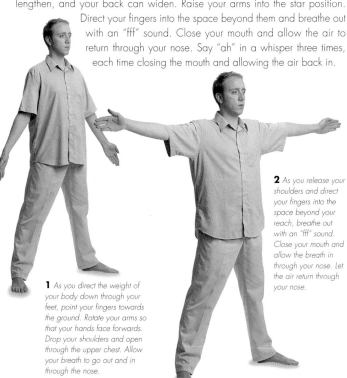

2 As you release your shoulders and direct your fingers into the space beyond your reach, breathe out with an "fff" sound. Close your mouth and allow the breath in through your nose. Let the air return through your nose.

1 As you direct the weight of your body down through your feet, point your fingers towards the ground. Rotate your arms so that your hands face forwards. Drop your shoulders and open through the upper chest. Allow your breath to go out and in through the nose.

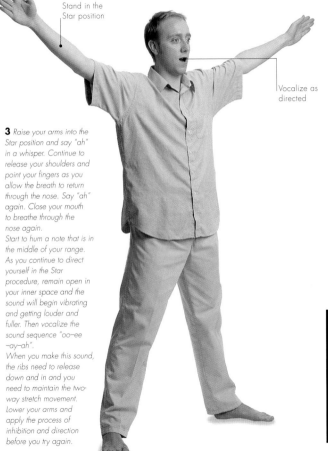

Stand in the
Star position

Vocalize as
directed

3 *Raise your arms into the
Star position and say "ah"
in a whisper. Continue to
release your shoulders and
point your fingers as you
allow the breath to return
through the nose. Say "ah"
again. Close your mouth
to breathe through the
nose again.*

*Start to hum a note that is in
the middle of your range.
As you continue to direct
yourself in the Star
procedure, remain open in
your inner space and the
sound will begin vibrating
and getting louder and
fuller. Then vocalize the
sound sequence "oo–ee
–ay–ah".*

*When you make this sound,
the ribs need to release
down and in and you
need to maintain the two-
way stretch movement.
Lower your arms and
apply the process of
inhibition and direction
before you try again.*

Stand Tall to Walk Forwards

Walking freely
Your teacher will remind you that the release of your knees will take you forwards freely.

Walking forwards enables you to achieve your goals and to attain what is needed to sustain life – food, shelter, and companionship. The human body is beautifully designed to co-ordinate the act of lengthening in a vertical direction with forward movement.

When you walk, the extent to which you naturally co-ordinate these requirements is evident in the economy and grace of your movement.

Response to time pressure
During the day you are faced with numerous stimuli that insist you move faster than is comfortable (or indeed faster than you are capable of) to get from one place to another in a hurry. Demands that require you to respond quickly cause you to over-flex the strong muscles of your body, shorten the muscles of the front, and restrict your breathing. When your body loses its natural movement into the vertical, your legs relinquish their natural spring and become stiff and less efficient at carrying your body forwards.

Stop and release
The inhibitory process helps you to break the habit of over-reacting to the need to move forwards to do things. By

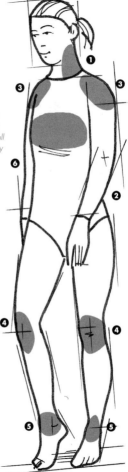

Be Aware

1 Neck free

2 Back lengthened

3 Shoulders released

4 Knees free to go forwards

5 Ankles free

6 Regular breathing

Walking tall
Walking forwards freely requires that you maintain the full length of your body into the upright.

stopping, you briefly detach yourself from the pressures of the environment and your end-gaining tendency, enabling you to release your neck and the tension down the front of your body. The directions help you to lengthen and widen and establish your full stature in the vertical plane. Lengthening helps to release the joints of the leg so that when you decide to walk forwards, there are no restrictions in the ankles, knees, and hips. Walking should be a pleasurable activity that enables us to progress. The release of your knee will then carry you forward easily and energetically.

WALKING FORWARDS

Before you walk forwards stop, release your neck, and lengthen up to your head and down to your feet. Be aware of what is going on around you, remaining alert and ready for the unexpected. Move with a natural rhythm in which your head is leading your body and your legs are moving along under you like the wheels of a bicycle. If you need to speed up, make sure that you allow your knees to release and that you continue to lengthen as you move forwards.

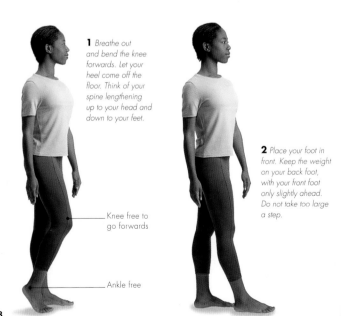

1 *Breathe out and bend the knee forwards. Let your heel come off the floor. Think of your spine lengthening up to your head and down to your feet.*

Knee free to go forwards

Ankle free

2 *Place your foot in front. Keep the weight on your back foot, with your front foot only slightly ahead. Do not take too large a step.*

Release your
neck to look
into the space
in front of you

3 *Let your head move over
your front foot and transfer
your weight forwards.
Release your back knee
forwards and allow your
heel to come off the ground.
Try not to move from side to
side, but continue in an
easy, flowing rhythm.*

Body
lengthens to
move
forwards

The Art of Running Freely

On your marks
If you free your neck, you release the explosive potential in your muscles, enabling a speedy take-off.

Running, like walking, demands two-way movement for efficient performance. Lengthening helps to release your joints, and reduces the pressure on your legs, so that your knees are free. A long spine ensures that you do not pound on your legs with each stride. By keeping leg work to a minimum, you will not tire as quickly. Keeping your neck free enables the arm and leg opposite each other to be connected through the back and co-ordinated, allowing the two sides of the body – left arm/right leg and right arm/left leg – to work as two springs. As one side works, the other side springs forwards. This helps your running to be light, free-flowing, and rhythmic.

Pushing yourself
Running starts as pure enjoyment – watch children revel in it before the competitive urge starts to take over. More and more people are attempting to run longer distances and working hard to better their times. At some point, you may start to suffer from one of the many running-related leg injuries such as Achilles' tendonitis, runner's knee, shin splints or muscle strain. Injury is often due to trying too hard in some way. Perhaps you over-engage the muscles that shorten your body, causing you to make too much impact with the ground. Your Alexander teacher can help you to understand why your movement creates injuries and help you rediscover the joy of running.

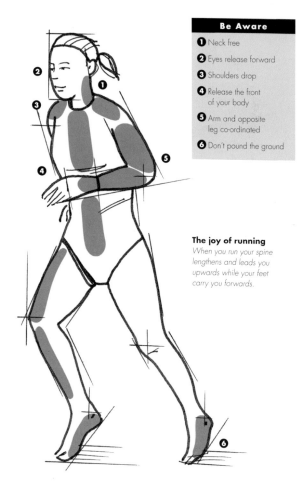

Be Aware

1. Neck free
2. Eyes release forward
3. Shoulders drop
4. Release the front of your body
5. Arm and opposite leg co-ordinated
6. Don't pound the ground

The joy of running

When you run your spine lengthens and leads you upwards while your feet carry you forwards.

RUN FOR ENJOYMENT

In order to run well, you need to lengthen as you make the effort to go forwards. It is important to listen to the feedback from your body during activity and recognize the signals that tell you when you are becoming inefficient, such as muscular tensions that contract your body and make your movements heavy. Alternatively, your stride length may become so long that it forces you to shorten your body, or you may resort to gasping or struggling to breathe in. These are signals that the forward impulse has interfered with your balance and freedom in the upright, a primary requirement if your movement is going to be easy, flowing, and rhythmic. Think about how you are running rather than the finishing line.

1 *Keep your elbows at a right angle and your wrists and hands firm but free. The action of drawing the elbow back thrusts the other side forwards.*

2 *Keep your neck free so that your head is balanced. Concentrate on lengthening up and look ahead.*

3 *Allow your knee to release forwards and your foot to roll on to your toes, preparing for the spring of your foot to thrust your leg forwards.*

4 *Let the hinges of your legs work to carry you forwards. Don't let your desire for an increased stride length cause you to forget to run tall.*

Case Study: Mother and Son

Fulfilled potential

For Erica and Simon, the Alexander Technique brought the added benefit of self-empowerment.

Erica and her son Simon had come for lessons because they both suffered from recurrent problems that were affecting their ability to work. Erica found that she was getting exhausted too easily and young Simon, after a rapid growing phase, was beginning to slump and not do as well as predicted. Erica was 42, with a highly-developed, sensitive nature, and prone to depression. She was intensely self-critical, which she covered by a happy-go-lucky attitude. Inclined to race through all activities, she was mentally, physically, and spiritually drained.

Son

Simon had inherited Erica's end-gaining tendencies and at 11 was very impatient to excel without putting in the necessary hard work. Both of them had a practically non-existent ability to stop. Simon also had a tendency to give up just as the end of any task was approaching. This problem was clearly evident on Sports Day, when he would pull back as the finishing line came in sight. His athletic prowess was not in question, but his commitment to finishing the task in hand needed some development.

Empowerment

As soon as Erica began to employ the concept of inhibition, she found that taking this time for herself gave great benefit. As her ability to say "No" improved, she began to make changes, not only in her psychophysical self, but also in responding to unreasonable demands on her time. In Simon's case, the ability to give directions freed him from the disorganized state in which he often found himself. By stopping and remembering to free his neck, he was empowered to continue with what needed to be done. He began to really enjoy competing, seeing it as a race against himself rather than an end-gaining exercise. Together they shared the experience of changing and their relationship, which had always been very close, improved and deepened. For them, practising the Alexander Technique became synonymous with empowering themselves.

Learning Together

There is much joy to be shared by family members as they open up to change.

SELF-MASTERY

The Alexander Technique helps you to relate two very powerful resources, which you may not be aware that you possess. These are self-awareness and making choices, and they operate at the most basic level of functioning. Every time you make a move, physically, mentally, or spiritually, you have the choice of working either for yourself or against yourself. Your response to life benefits from being under your control, helping you in everyday tasks, health maintenance, taking exercise, and at work. When you start to use these resources, you begin to master yourself.

Change Starts from Within

Patience
The simplest and most mundane tasks provide the opportunity for transformation.

changed. You can change your outward circumstances but ultimately, after the thrill of a new environment has worn off, you are once again left with yourself. The Christian mystic Thomas à Kempis said, "Give me the strength to change what can be changed, the ability to accept what cannot and the wisdom to tell the difference between them." Living according to these principles can be the beginning of greater self-acceptance and the basis for a more fulfilling life.

Change based on an inability or refusal to accept yourself and your faults will be difficult and uncomfortable. Sufi masters have said that the greatest freedom is the ability to accept that there is no freedom, that ultimately there are certain basic things about ourselves and life that cannot be

Learning how to stop

Two early publications on Alexander's work 'Knowing How to Stop' and 'The Man Who Mastered Habit' are testaments to his insight into the process of changing, making choices, and personal growth. These two small books contain some very important discoveries. The two simple concepts of habit and the ability to stop are discussed as a basis for growth. Change can be an

unsatisfactory process of imposing
something on yourself, and attempting to
shoehorn yourself into a way of
existence that isn't quite you. However,
when you understand how to stop, it
allows you to see yourself as you really
are, and shows you that transformation
really is possible.

Taking charge

Lessons in the Alexander Technique help
you to gain practical experience of your
ability to stop and show you that you
can use it to take charge of yourself. An
understanding of stopping is not
something to be acquired from outside,
but is an inherent part of your make-up
and provides a real basis from which
your journey of acceptance and
mastery of yourself can move forwards.

Getting Results

The principle of stopping makes great sense,
but the practical application of it is not
always easy.

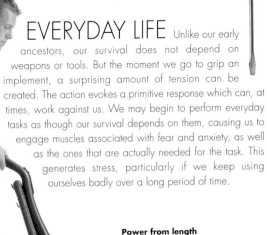

EVERYDAY LIFE

Unlike our early ancestors, our survival does not depend on weapons or tools. But the moment we go to grip an implement, a surprising amount of tension can be created. The action evokes a primitive response which can, at times, work against us. We may begin to perform everyday tasks as though our survival depends on them, causing us to engage muscles associated with fear and anxiety, as well as the ones that are actually needed for the task. This generates stress, particularly if we keep using ourselves badly over a long period of time.

Power from length
A lengthened spine releases forward energy, to help you push the vacuum cleaner across the carpet.

Enjoy your leisure
Some skills require your potential for finely tuned balance and co-ordination.

Balance
When carrying bags of shopping, release upwards and drop your shoulders to support the weight.

Hard work
Realize the extent to which the end-gaining tendency takes over, and apply the processes of inhibition and direction.

Exercise Consciously

Running free
*By using conscious control, ease
and grace of movement can be
available to all mankind.*

Vertebrates are designed so that movement is most efficient when it is the result of leading with the head and lengthening and widening in stature. Obeying these principles ensures that optimum breathing keeps the body well supplied with oxygen.

When you observe animals and skilled athletes, you notice that they lengthen in stature when they move. This is necessary if muscles are going to be used efficiently, without excessive strain or injury. Two fundamental principles are involved: focused attention, and expansion into full, extended movement through lengthening and widening.

Pushing yourself too hard

When you move or exercise, it is important to practise these primary principles of movement and locomotion. We start exercising in order to achieve some very clear goals. These may include getting fit, losing weight, or regaining muscle tone after years of indulgence. But determination to achieve targets may exaggerate the end-gaining tendency. You extend the stretch further, lift heavier weights, and run faster. The faster you move and the harder you work, the less able you are to get feedback from your body, and the danger of putting your body under too much strain is increased. It is important to be aware that developing muscles at the wrong pace can start to be counterproductive and damaging to health.

Feedback

Scientific study of exercise has confirmed that, although a certain amount of exercise can help keep us healthy, there is a point where exercise may suppress rather than enhance the immune system. The idea of achieving peak performance by exercising the body into exhaustion and then letting it recover is being questioned by both sports experts and scientists. It is not just a matter of how much exercise we do, but of how we work out.

Learning to exercise consciously means becoming more willing to pay attention to the signals from your body. Body use and breathing are the two primary indicators. They give you the feedback that will help you evaluate how much exercise leads you to end-gain to the extent that your exercise actually creates stress.

Head–neck–back
Your Alexander Technique teacher will suggest that you do not hold your head out of the water and will ask you to pay attention to your head–neck–back relationship.

SWIMMING
This is one of the best forms of exercise for the whole body. Clinical tests have recorded significant reductions in cardiovascular activity and levels of blood pressure. Practise by standing at the side of the pool holding on to the rail. Exhale first through your mouth only, then submerge both your mouth and nose, and finally your whole face. When you feel confident and relaxed about putting your whole face underwater, let go of the rail and glide forwards. As you become less self-conscious, you will develop a new way of swimming.

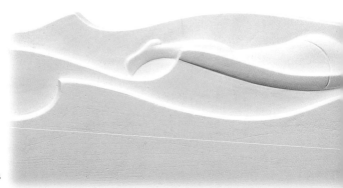

Supported by water

Water, which is a thousand times denser than air, bears the weight of your vertebrae and allows more release in your muscles.

Swimming well

When you free your neck, you will be able to float higher and move with greater ease. Your attention should be on the exhalation of breath, so that inhalation happens automatically.

Riding

In the Spanish Riding School in Vienna, considered to be one of the finest places for equestrian training, men and horses are schooled together. Experienced riders are placed on young horses and young riders are placed on experienced horses. In this way, they learn from each other.

Riding demands a conscious awareness of self. If you do not have the alert stillness described earlier in the book, the results can be disastrous. Animals, as we have seen, operate in a very well-ordered, instinctive way. Horses are quick to recognize any lack of control or disorganization in human behaviour. Anyone who is frightened of being in the saddle will, more often than not, end up on the ground fairly quickly. The Alexander Technique, through its ability to bring about conscious postural use and some control of the fear reflex, enables progress to be made. Good posture is one of the fundamental requirements for any rider. Practise the posture required for riding prior to mounting your horse.

Riding posture

Begin by standing upright, applying the principles of the Alexander Technique, then place your feet about 60 centimetres (2 feet) apart. Allow your head to nod forwards, and bend your knees slightly. You should be able to maintain the posture without undue effort. Practising this posture will make it easier for you to keep your balance once you have got on the horse.

Sit comfortably in the saddle, making a good contact through your seat bones. When the horse first moves forwards, problems often begin. As a rider, you have a lot to think about – your own state and that of your horse. Suddenly, you find yourself falling forwards or backwards, and having to grab the reins for support. The use of your hands needs to be conscious, directed, sensitive, and without undue body movement. There should be an almost mystical union between horse and rider, providing an excellent example of human and equine proprioception working together.

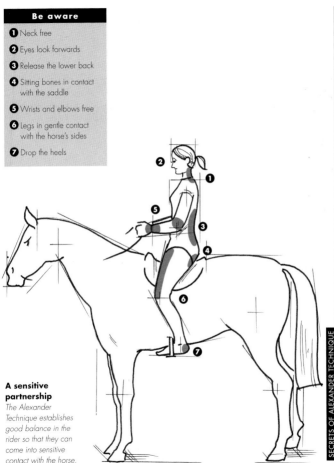

Be aware

1. Neck free
2. Eyes look forwards
3. Release the lower back
4. Sitting bones in contact with the saddle
5. Wrists and elbows free
6. Legs in gentle contact with the horse's sides
7. Drop the heels

A sensitive partnership

The Alexander Technique establishes good balance in the rider so that they can come into sensitive contact with the horse.

BALANCED RIDING

To ride well, you need to master a wide range of skills such as balance, sensitivity, controlled strength, suppleness, and, crucially, empathy with the animal on which you are seated. It is proprioception in action. Posture is absolutely critical, because the synchronized use of the back, seat, legs, and hands has a powerful influence on the animal beneath you. A horse cannot be forced to perform a movement, but it can be persuaded to do so. By applying the Alexander principles and sitting in a balanced way, riding can be effortless.

Chair

When the rider's body is behind the vertical, the reins will be used for support. The rider will assume the chair seat; rigid and stiff with the feet stuck forward.

Balanced

The rider's body is upright, with the knees slightly bent. The loins are gently braced, with the feet placed correctly in the stirrups.

Forked

When the rider's body is in front of the vertical, the shoulders tend to round, causing the feet to slip backward and lifting the rider's seat from the saddle.

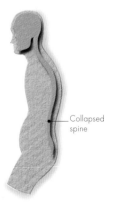

Collapsed spine

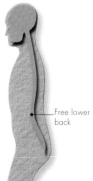

Free lower back

Over-arched

Unity

*Riders and their mounts, when
performing at their best, seem to
be one entity. Harmony is so
complete that the horse will
respond to the merest touch, or
even thought, from its rider.*

Tai Chi

Spinal vertebrae

Natural spring

The quality of movement is such that the length and inherent spring of the spine can be maintained as the basis of going into movement.

Tai chi comprises a sequence of non-stop movements, known as "the form", which developed in China hundreds of years ago as a system of self-defence and self-development. The various exercises that make up the form were designed to promote health and longevity and to cultivate a deeper awareness of mind–body potential.

The movements in a tai chi form appear effortless, yet they require great concentration and muscular energy. To be correctly executed, each movement requires a particular body posture, which focuses attention on the movement sequence.

Two disciplines

Both tai chi and the Alexander Technique aim to restore the flexibility and balance that is our natural birthright; they also view the body and mind as a united whole which requires training. The disciplines are different, but their intentions are the same.

In an Alexander lesson, you are encouraged to avoid end-gaining by inhibiting your habitual response to stimuli, to free your neck and let your head go forward and up and to focus on the means you use to reach a goal.

In a tai chi form, the student must quieten the mind and, with calm focus and with "a head balanced as if suspended from above", perform a prescribed series of movements. However, it is the quality of the movements and the way in which they are achieved that are significant, not the number of movements performed.

Common links

Slow movements allow time for sensory information to be conveyed from the brain into awareness. Fast movements do not permit time for feedback. Tai chi, with its emphasis on slow movements, is an excellent procedure for applying the awareness of balance and posture that is gained through learning the Alexander Technique.

Tai chi and the Alexander Technique therefore have a great deal in common, because both help in the achievement of good posture, easy breathing, relaxed and free movement, and general wellbeing. In addition, studying either system also imparts a practical knowledge of the skeleton, musculature, and general body mechanics, raising body awareness and instilling the balance and co-ordination required to perform any task efficiently and gracefully.

Yin and Yang

These are central to the practice of tai chi. They represent the dynamic union of opposing forces, for example light and dark.

The Yellow Emperor
Huang Di, the Yellow Emperor, is attributed with the authorship of the Neijing, one of the most important Taoist classics and the seminal theoretical treatise on traditional Chinese medicine.

YIN AND YANG IN MOVEMENT

Yin and yang represent the dynamic union of opposing forces such as light and dark, yielding and active, feminine and masculine. Tai chi is composed of constant polarities, such as open and closed movements. The aim of each movement is to restore perfect equilibrium between yin and yang. In the Alexander Technique, inhibition corresponds to the passive principle (yin), direction the active (yang). Each facilitates the other – without each other they are meaningless. By following this principle in both systems, the proprioceptive sense is gradually cultivated, allowing a greater sense of the position of the body relative to the space it inhabits and to itself.

Meditation in motion
The tai chi form is a constant round of symmetry and transformation. Each movement is replaced by another movement in a continuous, flowing cycle.

Grasp Sparrow's Tail

This posture grounds the body through the earth, feet, and pelvis, with most weight down through the right foot. Attention is on the hands, as if gathering energy.

Focus, control, and balance are the objects of this exercise

Left hand turns outwards

Single whip

This posture develops focus, control and balance. The hooked right hand anchors the body, holding and redistributing the energy to the left hand which turns from palm facing the body to palm away. As it does so, awareness moves outward, away from the body, and the lungs open fully.

Pregnancy and Childbirth

Feeling the strain

The growing foetus presses on the heart, lungs, and other internal organs, often causing digestive problems or breathing difficulties.

During pregnancy, a woman's body undergoes a bewildering number of physical and psychological changes. As hormones flood through her, affecting her emotionally, her body is adapting to accommodate the foetus within. As the baby grows, the increased weight at the front shifts her centre of balance. The woman's usual instinct is to lean back from the waist to compensate for the extra weight she has to carry. In doing this, she puts untold pressure on the lower back and sacrum, resulting in chronic back pain.

An Alexander teacher will show a pregnant woman how to expand her torso and release pressure from the spinal area, redistributing the baby's weight through her body. This protects the back and alleviates restriction of the internal organs, allowing her to breathe freely. The weight of the baby also affects the woman's range and ease of movement. Simple everyday tasks such as bending, lifting, carrying, standing, and sitting become increasingly difficult or uncomfortable. The sooner a pregnant woman begins lessons in the Alexander Technique, the better. It takes time to replace ingrained patterns of muscular tension. Having learnt to exercise conscious control over posture and movement, the woman can apply this skill to her daily life and also, crucially, prepare for childbirth itself.

Childbirth

For most women, the instinctive response to pain is to tense the whole body and hold the breath, and this is compounded by the *expectation* of pain with each contraction, leading to anxiety. Anxiety, in turn, releases all the wrong hormones and may halt or delay the birthing process. Similarly, the use of painkilling drugs confuses the body's signals and may result in the need for medical intervention.

The Whispered "Ah" exercise is beneficial when a contraction is due. Alexander's instruction for dealing with anxiety was to think of something funny and smile. The act of smiling releases tension in the jaw and face, causing the salivary glands to secrete saliva. Saliva sends a message to the brain that all is well and there is no need for anxiety.

Happy together
The Alexander Technique helps you to deal with the demands of raising a young family.

CHILDBIRTH

The Alexander Technique can play a critical role in natural childbirth. It teaches that pain is a necessary part of labour. During the first stage, as the cervix dilates, the mother is encouraged just to allow the process to happen. With each subsequent contraction she is encouraged to move, to breathe freely, and practise the Whispered "Ah" exercise. Freedom of movement is necessary to ease pain, but by using the Alexander directions, the woman can practise crawling, squatting, kneeling, or bending – whichever posture feels "right" for her, in order to assist delivery.

Bending

The dynamic posture of bending is particularly effective during pregnancy and childbirth. As the mother leans forwards in this position, the baby is cushioned by her abdominal wall while her pelvis tilts, encouraging the baby to move into the correct position for delivery. Simultaneously, the baby's weight, working with the force of gravity, initiates stronger and more efficient contractions.

Squatting

Squatting puts a dynamic stretch through the whole back. This posture helps to lengthen out the muscles of the lower back in particular, and to relieve muscles that may have over-contracted whilst supporting the baby.

Crawling

Crawling is highly beneficial as a preparation for childbirth, since many women find it more comfortable to be on all fours during labour. Crawling also helps calm the nerves, alleviate minor aches and pains and improve co-ordination.

Leading with the head, crawl slowly forwards

Repeat several times, then rest on all fours, gently rocking the body

Kneel on all fours, fingers pointing forwards

The "steps" should be small and rhythmical: left hand and right knee, then right hand and left knee, and so on

ALEXANDER TECHNIQUE

187

A Healthy Mind and Body

Psychosomatic illness

Many medical conditions can result from normal stress responses being over-activated.

The term "psychosomatic" recognizes that there is a profound relationship between psychological experience and physiological functioning. Alexander was ahead of his time in realizing that the mind and body are not separate entities, but different aspects of the self.

Wellbeing

When you have a sense of wellbeing, is it a physical or a mental experience? When you are at ease, mind and body are in a state of equilibrium. If something were to change in the organism as a whole, then both mind and body would reflect that. Depression involves a collapse of your body, a lowering of energy, and a lowering of self-esteem. When threatened, you prepare to defend yourself by tensing your muscles, your blood sugar rises, and your pulse rate increases. If, for some reason, you are anxious about expressing your aggression, the level of muscular tension may increase, reflecting that resistance. When people cannot decide between alternatives or have a conflict of interests that pull them in two directions, they can "freeze". Listening to the voice of conscience is no less physiological than mastering a manual skill is an act of mindful attention.

Preventing trouble

Many medical conditions are the result of normal stress responses being over-activated. When allowed to continue, they interfere with recovery of the whole mind and body, and can, over time, lead to illness. Alexander emphasized that he did not treat specific symptoms and stressed the preventive nature of his work. However, he did recognize that misuse was an underlying factor in disease and by establishing a better use of the self, functioning improved and specific symptoms often disappeared. Similar observations led Nikolas Tinbergen, the 1973 winner of the Nobel prize for medicine, to "...recommend the Alexander Technique as an extremely sophisticated form of rehabilitation of the entire muscular equipment and through that of many other organs showing very striking improvements in such diverse things as high blood pressure, breathing, depth of sleep, and overall cheerfulness."

COPING WITH ARTHRITIS

When an arthritic condition is related to repeated pressure on a joint, the Alexander Technique can help to alleviate pain and facilitate mobility. Sufferers tend to focus exclusively on the area that is inflamed and painful, but an Alexander teacher's approach will be to encourage attention to general muscular co-ordination and away from the area where the symptom is present. The teacher will guide the use of the whole body in such a way that it re-establishes its natural support, counteracting any tendency to a collapsed or rigid posture that will exert unnecessary pressure on the joint in question. In an Alexander lesson, you experience the muscles of the body working together as an intricately connected whole. As your sensory appreciation improves, you can be more aware of the role of the misuse of the primary control and the pressure being put on specific joints, which it is important to be aware of if you suffer from arthritis.

Pain management
Arthritis is a painful condition. Your Alexander teacher will try to help you to avoid over-tightening in response to the pain.

Wear and tear

When a door on a hinge is pressed down, the action is rather like what happens when a joint is pressed down: extra friction is created.

Easy does it

The pressure on your joints created by lifting a heavy object will be aggravated by over-contraction prior to movement. Applying the process of inhibition and direction before lifting a heavy object releases your joints and lengthens your muscles in preparation for the task ahead.

Healthy Breathing and a Healthy Heart

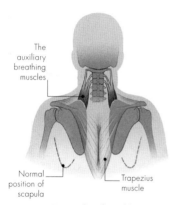

The auxiliary breathing muscles

Normal position of scapula

Trapezius muscle

Upper chest breathing
When the diaphragm cannot move normally and breathing is difficult, the neck and shoulders tighten to assist breathing.

The connection between anxiety, postural change, and altered breathing patterns may be an underlying factor in breathing disorders. The physical response to stress or anxiety is a shortening of the body and an increase in the respiratory–metabolic rate. This has its basis in established patterns of animal behaviour, where it is advantageous to become smaller to hide from danger or predators, and simultaneously increase the metabolic rate and the readiness of muscles in preparation for fight or flight.

Normal breathing depends on whether the body is well-balanced and maintained at its full height with minimum effort. The diaphragm is the principal muscle for breathing in and accounts for 60–80 per cent of the movement of the ribcage and lungs in a healthy individual. If you are slumped or collapsed, the lack of internal space restricts the action of the diaphragm.

Over-constriction

Equally, if you are over-contracted, there is an active resistance created in your body to the movement of the ribcage, making it impossible for the diaphragm to move the ribcage normally. Extra muscular effort is then required to overcome the resistance. These muscles serve to lift the shoulders and help the external muscles of the chest work to draw air into the lungs.

This pattern of a raised upper chest is often present in people with asthma, and can be found in those with high blood pressure, hypertension, and coronary problems. A raised upper chest makes breathing out difficult. The excessive effort used to breathe in sets up tensions which prevent the relaxation of the chest that happens in normal exhalation. Breathing in naturally requires that you first breathe out, but if you are holding your breath, you will struggle for your next breath. The harder you work to breathe in, the less likely you are to want to breathe out. In this way, holding and struggling for breath becomes an established pattern. The Alexander Technique can help in this situation, because you become aware of all the factors that are working together to create the tensions that result in restricted breathing.

Recovering from injury
After an injury, too much inactivity leads to loss of elasticity in the muscles, making you vulnerable to injury when you resume action.

INJURY AND PAIN

Posture plays an important part in pain management and in rehabilitation following injury. To protect the injured area and avoid increased pain, you compensate and adjust your posture, often putting increased pressure on the affected area. Perhaps you are simply careful in your movements, in order to guard against any activity that will set off the pain again. This is likely to increase the blood flow to the injured area, leading to further muscle spasm and pain. If you are immobilized altogether, the decreased activity in your muscles leads to loss of elasticity. Loss of elasticity is a common pattern in many conditions of the muscles and joints. This makes you vulnerable to injury when you resume activity. You oscillate between over-tight muscles or atrophied muscles and collapse. The Alexander Technique increases your awareness and helps you manage the relationship between the use of your whole body and the freedom and mobility of specific joints. It encourages you to feel the connection between your attitude and the injury you have sustained.

Adding to injury
When you are in pain your whole body tightens. In your attempt to avoid pain, you unintentionally put more pressure on the injured area.

Do not
over-tighten the
injured area

Dealing with Depression

Blue mood
Posture has a profound effect on you. Changing your posture and encouraging natural breathing can help lift depression.

In attempting to understand the origins of depression, some psychiatrists have identified evolutionary factors and argue that various mechanisms have evolved to enable us to deal with loss. When loss, defeat, or subordination occur, an involuntary process comes into play, resulting in a change in posture, a lowering of energy, a change in mood, poor appetite, laziness of movement, and loss of confidence. These changes signal to an aggressor that the antagonist has submitted and assure him that further attack is not likely. The lowering of energy helps the vanquished animal signal defeat and accept it, ensuring that a thoughtless attempt at a comeback, in which there would be a risk of death, does not happen. These responses ensure that disputes are settled quickly, reduce unnecessary aggressiveness within groups, and ensure harmony within clearly established social strata. Once the dispute is over, animals tend to recover their equilibrium and respectfully adopt their position in the group hierarchy.

Depression in humans often follows loss or defeat of some kind. Love, affection, companionship, status, and group recognition are critical factors in health and wellbeing, and a loss in any one of these areas can trigger the onset of a depressive episode. In cases of mild depression, there is much that can be done through self-help. By recognizing the extent to which the depression is an old pattern, and that you may be perpetuating it, you have reached a point of change.

Turning the corner

Using the process of inhibition enables you to listen to the signals from your depression and be honest about your active role in it. When your body adopts a depressed stance, your breathing becomes limited. Practise the Whispered "Ah" exercise in the star position to help yourself out of your slumped posture and re-energize your breath. Your posture has a profound effect on you. Becoming conscious of your movement has been found useful in helping you shift your mood. Changing your posture and encouraging natural breathing opens the possibility for you to play a more proactive role in your psychophysical state.

When to Get Medical Help

Severe depression requires medical help. In less serious cases, the Alexander Technique is beneficial to the long process of recovery.

UPPER LIMB DISORDERS

Repetitive strain injury (RSI) is now referred to in the *British Medical Journal* as work-related upper limb disorder. The problem commonly occurs in wrists, fingers, and forearms, when the tendon or the sheath of the tendon become inflamed. Activities such as racquet sports, which demand repetitive movements of the wrists, or typing and word processing, which demand repetitive finger movements, are liable to produce this condition. Reducing the stress on the muscles, tendons, and joints can help with this debilitating disorder. Recent research suggests that injury can result from pushing the brain beyond its capacity to manage fast, precise movements. Treatment for the condition has tended to involve resting or immobilizing the limb. If the research is correct, the Alexander Technique, which re-awakens feeling and helps the brain to relearn control of precise movement, would be more appropriate.

Awareness in action
The Alexander Technique heightens sensory feedback and improves control of your body and your instrument.

Fast and furious

Excessive pressure on the joints and pushing the brain beyond its capacity to manage fast, precise movements can lead to problems in your joints and limbs. Remember to maintain the two-way stretch of your back muscles. Take frequent breaks and point your fingers to the ground to allow a lengthening of your muscles, and to relieve the pressure around your joints.

Tight neck

Braced hands

Over-flexing throughout the body

Emotion, Posture, and Digestion

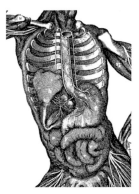

Improved digestion
Many people have found that their digestion improves as a result of lessons in the Alexander Technique.

Many doctors believe that gastrointestinal conditions can be stress-related, and that our ability to digest food is affected by tension, anxiety, and other emotional factors. The relationship between the fight or flight response and digestive function is essential to the survival of animals in the wild. Mild fear causes an involuntary muscle contraction in the descending colon. When mild fear turns to panic, the contents of the intestines are liquefied and the animal involuntarily evacuates just before it breaks into flight. Mild fear appears to be associated with constipation, and terror with diarrhoea. This suggests that normal reactions to fear could lead to intestinal disorders in humans. Perhaps the increased pace and pressure of life are evoking survival responses leading to digestive problems.

Many people have found that their digestion improves as a result of lessons in the Alexander Technique. Posture, emotion, and digestion are so intimately connected that the combined effect of re-establishing balance and relieving emotional pressure can bring immediate benefit. An appropriate level of tension in the abdomen is important for digestion – too much or too little may lead to poor intestinal functioning.

Some people react to stress in a way that causes tension in the abdomen. Improving posture helps to remove pressure from the abdomen and to achieve the abdominal tone necessary for good digestion.

Indigestible facts

A high level of tension is often the result of fear or some other strong emotion. An acute attack of indigestion may follow an incident that produced rage or fear. Perhaps a tendency to rush about confuses the body into thinking that something is wrong and the fear response is activated without our being aware of it.

Current fashion extols the virtues of a flat stomach. Too much tension in the abdomen restricts intestinal functioning. When you hold your stomach in, the ribcage responds by becoming fixed. If the ribcage cannot move, excess pressure is put on the stomach and may lead to indigestion.

THE WHOLE PERSON

Certain flowers are used as symbols of the obstacles that life presents, the predisposition to overcome them, and the inevitability of growth and spiritual unfolding. In the East it is the lotus, in the West, the rose and the lily. The seed is the concentration of potential, and the bud, rising from the darkness in the earth and responding to light, overcomes the force of gravity, expanding and opening outwards. It reveals its inner beauty through the unfolding of its petals and, as its perfume escapes, it allows its essence to be expressed in the world. Achieving your full posture could be likened to the flowering and unfolding of yourself. Just as you are programmed to counteract the downward force of gravity, similarly you are predisposed to overcome obstacles and realize your potential. You and your posture are deeply intertwined. The Alexander Technique helps you to understand the patterns and behaviour of your body, sometimes deeply ingrained, and how they express your relationship to yourself and your response to life.

Reach for the stars

The relationship between the attainment of full stature and the achievement of potential is captured in this drawing by Leonardo da Vinci.

Self-realization
Postural awareness helps bring about a flowering and unfolding of yourself.

Mind–body balance
"When the mind is free, the body is delicate."
WILLIAM SHAKESPEARE

Integrating Instinct, Emotion, and Reason

Stillness
Stopping opens up the dialogue between thoughts and feelings.

Numerous human responses originate in animal behaviour. Many of the patterns that some consider to be neurotic are actually remnants of responses that were biologically useful throughout evolution. Experiences of fear and anxiety were crucial for survival and found response

in flight, attack, submission, and "freezing". The management of aggression is a major factor in human evolution and social organization. The role of the front brain allows control of charged emotional responses and brings a rational perspective into the equation. However, this is a relatively recent development and often the presence of reason simply suppresses the feedback from feelings, thereby increasing conflict and causing the aggression to be turned inwards. You experience a "frozen" response, revealing the struggle between instinct, emotion, and reason. The purpose of inhibition is to open up the dialogue between feeling and reason, so that your choices can be an expression of an undivided self.

Constant stimuli

In many ways, life is getting easier for humans. However, an improvement in opportunities brings new and unexpected problems. Overpopulation, overcrowding, the pace of life, material expectations, dreams of happy relationships, and fame all contribute to making humans feel overpowered by increasing external needs. These factors may have the effect of arousing (on a subliminal level) the competitive response – of assessing strength, evaluating the capacity for success or failure, and activation of the fight or flight response (either in a state of arousal and attack, or retreat and defeat). By helping you to become more sensitive to the working of your upright posture, the Alexander Technique enables you to become more aware of the power of expectations and your responses to stimuli such as fear, anxiety, or a constant state of anticipation.

Changing Focus

Inhibition enables you to suspend the attraction of the external environment and shift your attention to the importance of inner life.

PERFORMANCE ANXIETY

In everyday life, the fight or flight response can be unexpectedly aroused by situations that cause worry or anxiety, causing tension and an increase in heart rate and breathing. Animals instinctively decide between alternatives, and either retreat from that which they find frightening, or turn and fight. Humans, with their evolved brains, are conscious that their instinctive response can be inappropriate. However, acting against one's impulses, or having to decide between irreconcilable alternatives, can cause anxiety, stress, and muscular tension. These patterns may be compounded if you doubt your abilities, or if the things you want are in conflict with the things you feel are possible. The Alexander Technique helps you to manage these responses.

Directed energy

Performance requires an increase in energy. There is a fine line betweeen excitement and anxiety. The Alexander Technique helps you to understand the difference.

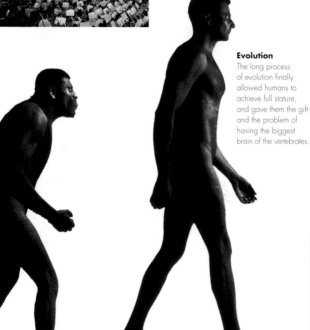

Evolution

The long process of evolution finally allowed humans to achieve full stature, and gave them the gift and the problem of having the biggest brain of the vertebrates.

Working with Children

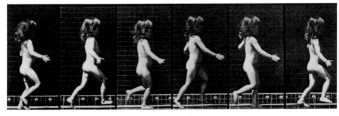

Dancing for joy
*The poise and freedom of movement
shown by children is a natural ability
often lost as they get older.*

Children have a natural curiosity about their environment. As parents, the challenge is to allow children to explore the world whilst preventing them from coming to any harm. When children leave the supervision of parents to play with other children or to go to school, they enter a competitive world and from time to time may become threatened by the new society or the challenge of learning new skills, perhaps because their sense of self-esteem is questioned. Sometimes parents have to judge carefully when to challenge and encourage their children, and when to let them follow their instinct to stay sheltered in the safety of the home. Often parents have unreasonable expectations of their children, perhaps rooted in their own failures and uncertainties. All children copy the habits, both positive and negative, of the people who are looking after them, so it is important to reinforce focus and calmness rather than aggressive responses and panic.

Give love unconditionally

When the giving of love is made conditional on sporting and academic success, children can become unsure of themselves. They are no longer motivated by curiosity and interest, but by a fear that if they fail they will not be loved. Feelings of unworthiness and frustration start to shroud their natural freedom and they begin to try to get things right in order to prove themselves. Anger and impatience on the part of adults will only aggravate these insecurities, so that the the fight or fight reflex becomes over-stimulated and well-established.

Reinforce the positive

The predisposition to learn involves allowing time to absorb, evaluate, and digest information. It is important that adults have a feel for a child's learning cycle, then they can help reinforce learning without upsetting the process. This requires patience on the part of adults and the ability to apply their own conscious inhibition. It is pointless and discouraging to keep telling the child he is wrong. The continued reinforcement of the positive is an essential part of good training.

Good Parenting

When you greet young children, they usually respond joyfully, without disrupting freedom of movement. This is natural inhibition operating.

TEACHING CHILDREN

How often has the instruction "Stand up straight" been whispered, shouted, or simply mechanically requested by parents and teachers? When a child is sitting or standing in what you consider to be a slumped way, it is important that she is guided carefully and imaginatively to stand at her full height. If you order her to do it in a bossy, dictatorial manner, you are likely to activate her fight or flight response and encourage her to use a self-defeating way of trying to straighten her body. As it feels uncomfortable and unnatural, she will often abandon the attempt to stand up correctly. If it becomes a contentious issue, you may reinforce the habit of standing badly, because the child will begin to use her posture to make a statement about how she chooses to stand. As well as a physical stance, it becomes an emotional response. When children have the experience of standing at their full height, their movement patterns become more efficient, which reinforces their sense of achievement.

Ready for life

It is important to reinforce children's natural poise and innate sense of alert stillness from an early age.

Sense of play

Children display natural inhibition, energy, and flexibility, which, if lost, can be rediscovered through the Alexander Technique. Educators must be careful not to frustrate children's zest for living.

Wheeling through life

The joy of living, expressed in movement, is a wonderful thing, and can be enjoyed by young and old alike.

Children have a natural ease of movement

Realizing Your
True Potential

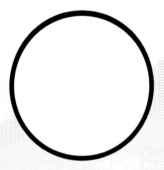

Empty space
*All possibilities are open to
you if you do not try too hard
to find them.*

outside world are more interesting than
those from within, but the danger of this
is that it sets up barriers against
knowledge from within. This may cause
you to disregard your intuitive response
to a situation.

Using the conscious mind
If you ignore your inner thoughts,
intuition, and information coming
from the outside world, you are not
using your conscious mind fully. The
conscious mind has a larger job to do,
including the examination of beliefs
and the assessment of experiences.
When you use your mind in this more
complete way, you become able to
make choices.

We possess two powerful
resources that we do not
tap to their full potential –
self-awareness, and choice. The
conscious mind is designed to receive
data from both the outside world and
the inner self. The information that
comes from the inner self requires time
for reflection and consideration. We
often assume that stimuli from the

Generally speaking psychological
imbalance happens in one of two
ways. On the one hand a belief or
sense of self has got into your pattern
that doesn't belong there. Or some part
of your inner process which should be
there has gone missing. The more the

conscious mind learns to pay attention, the more these patterns reveal themselves and become available for examination. During every moment of life you are in the process of either giving permission for something to continue or refusing to let something happen. The Alexander Technique invites you to bring this inevitable process up to the level of your conscious awareness and to direct its course. Take the chance to stop. In this way you can listen and gently release yourself. Perhaps new possibilities emerge or you see an old situation in a new light. Make a choice and follow your direction. As you experience your full height you may be released from your past and have the chance of a new beginning.

Alert Stillness

Inhibition and direction will help you establish a place of alert stillness from which you can make clear, considered moves.

GLOSSARY

Atlanto-occipital joint joint between bone at the base of the skull and the top vertebra of spinal column, which allows the head to nod.

Atrophy waste away.

Attitude i) position of the body, as suggesting some thought, feeling, or action; ii) state of mind, behaviour, or conduct.

Chronic a long-term or frequently recurring condition or disease that resists all efforts to eradicate it.

Collapse slump.

Conscious control faculty allowing for organization of responses to make choices in activity.

Cortical opposition action of placing first finger and thumb together.

Counterbalance power that equally opposes or balances another.

Diaphragm principal muscle used for breathing in, which separates the chest and abdominal cavities. It flattens out prior to breathing in.

Directions thought processes involved in sending instructions to encourage release, lengthening, and widening.

End-gaining tendency to focus on an end result while disregarding the process needed to achieve it.

Equilibrium balance.

Exhalation breathing air out of the lungs.

Extension act or process of straightening of a limb.

Facilitate make easier or more convenient.

Fibre fine strand of nerve or muscle tissue.

Habit established pattern or behavioural tendency.

Hyoid bone U-shaped bone at the base of the tongue.

Immune system the body's natural defences against disease.

Impulse i) natural, unreasoned motive or tendency to act; ii) desire to respond resulting from an instantaneous assessment of how to deal with a situation.

Inhibition decision to not respond to a stimulus.

Intercostal muscle muscle between the ribs.

Larynx organ of voice in the upper part of the trachea.

Means-whereby Alexander's term for the art of paying attention to how an end is achieved.

Misuse incorrect or inefficient way of working.

Pelvis part of the skeleton that forms a bony girdle joining the lower limbs to the body.

Physiology science of the functioning of living organisms.

Postural fibre muscle tissue that is capable of activity at very low levels of contraction for long periods of time.

Postural mechanisms mechanisms relating to balance and posture.

Posture attitude of the body.

Predisposition tendency, either innate or learnt, to think or respond in a particular way.

Primary control dynamic relationship between the head, neck, back, and breathing that influences the co-ordination of the rest of the body and is fundamental to human posture and movement.

Proprioception process of evaluating body position and noting muscle involvement.

Psychophysical the unity of mind and body.

Pulling down the action of contracting the body, and preventing working at full stature.

Reflex involuntary, unlearnt response to a stimulus.

Release free or liberate.

Respiration movement of air in and out of the lungs.

Retract draw back or shorten.

Sacrum fused lumbar vertebrae forming the lower part of vertebral column, together with the coccyx.

Semi-supine lying down with the head supported and legs bent, allowing the muscles of the body to release so that lengthening and widening occur.

Sensation change in state of awareness due to the stimulation of a nerve process, especially by those stimuli affecting any of the sense organs.

Sensory appreciation the ability to assess feedback from other senses, and an awareness of tension levels.

Spine backbone, made up of vertebrae.

Stimulus i) outside agent influencing activity of an organism; ii) initiation of impulse in nerve or muscle producing change in consciousness.

Tai chi sequence of non-stop movements, designed to promote health and longevity and to cultivate a deeper awareness of mind–body potential.

Torque anything that causes the body to twist or rotate.

Vertebrate animal with segmented spinal column.

Vocal folds voice-producing part of the larynx, formerly known as the vocal cords.

Yang (in Chinese philosophy) male principle. Source of life and heat.

Yin: (in Chinese philosophy) female principle. Stands for cold, darkness and death.

FURTHER READING

ALEXANDER, F. M., *Articles and Lectures*, compiled by Jean M. O. Fisher, Mouritz, London, 1995

ALEXANDER, F. M., *Constructive Conscious Control of the Individual*, STAT Books, London, 1997

ALEXANDER, F. M., *Man's Supreme Inheritance*, Mouritz, London, 1996

ALEXANDER, F. M., *The Use of the Self*, Gollancz, London, 1996

ALEXANDER, F. M., *The Universal Constant in Living*, Mouritz, London, 2000

BARLOW, W., (ed.), *More Talk of Alexander*, Gollancz, London, 1970, 1978

CARRINGTON, W., *The Act of Living*, edited by Jerry Sontag, Mornum Time Press, San Francisco, 1999

CARRINGTON, W., *Thinking Aloud*, edited by Jerry Sontag, Mornum Time Press, San Francisco, 1994

CARRINGTON, W. and CAREY, S., *Explaining the Alexander Technique: The Writings of F. Matthias Alexander*, The Sheldrake Press, London, 1992

DE ALACANTRA, P., *Indirect Procedures: A Musician's Guide to the Alexander Technique*, with a foreword by Sir Colin Davis, Oxford University Press, Oxford, 1997

GARLICK, D., *The Lost Sixth Sense, A Medical Scientist Looks at the Alexander Technique*, University of New South Wales, Kensington, 1990

GARLICK, D. (ed.), *Proprioception, Posture and Emotion*, University of New South Wales, Kensington, 1982

GELB, M., *Body Learning*, Aurum Press, 1981

JONES, F. P., *Freedom to Change: The Development and Science of the Alexander Technique*, Mouritz, London, 1997

JONES, F. P., BARLOW, W., HUXLEY, A., et al., *Knowing How to Stop, A Collection of Essays*, Chaterson, 1946

MACDONALD, G., *Alexander Technique*, Hodder & Stoughton, London, 1994

MACDONALD, G., *The Complete Illustrated Guide to Alexander Technique*, Element Books Ltd., Shaftesbury, 1998

MACDONALD, P., *The Alexander Technique (As I See It)*, Rahula Books, 1989

MACDONALD, R., *The Use of the Voice: Sensory Appreciation, Posture, Vocal Functioning and*

Shakespearean Text Performance, Macdonald Media, London, 1997

MACHOVER, I., DRAKE, A. AND DRAKE, J., *The Alexander Technique, Birth Book*, Sterling Publishing, New York, London, 1993, reissued as *Pregnancy and Birth the Alexander Way*, Robinson Publishing Ltd., London, 1995

SHAW, S. and D'ANGOUR, A., *The Art of Swimming*, Ashgrove Press Ltd., Bath, 1996

USEFUL ADDRESSES

**Alexander Training Voice
Communication
Macdonald Media Ltd.**
email: enquiries@macdonaldmedia.co.uk
www.macdonaldmedia.co.uk

**American Society for
the Alexander Technique**
(AmSAT – formerly NASTAT)
401 East Market Street
Charlottesville
VA 2290
Tel: 1 804 295 2840
(800 473 0620 toll free in US)
Fax: 1 804 295 3947
email: alexandertec@earthink.com
www.alexandertech.org

**Associaçào Brasileira
da Técnica Alexander (ABTA)**
Caixa Postal 16020
Rio de Janeiro
RJ Brazil
CEP 22220-970
Tel & Fax: 55 21 239 66 18
email:abta@montreal.com.br

**Assoc. Française des Prof.
Tecnique Alexander (APTA)**
42 Terrasse de l'Iris
La Défense 2, 92400
Courbevoie
France
Tel & Fax: 33 140 90 06 23
email: aptafr@aol.com

**Australian Society of Teachers of
the Alexander Technique (AUSTAT)**
P O Box 716
Darlinghurst NSW 2010
Australia
Tel: 1800 339 571(toll free number within
Australia)
email: ruthshoe@bigpond.com
www.alexandertechnique.org.au

**Belgian Assoc. of Teachers of F. M.
Alexander Technique (AEFMAT)**
4 Rue des Fonds,
B-1380 Lasne
Belgium
Tel & Fax: 32 2 633 3059
email: synergon@skynet.be

**The Canadian Society of Teachers
of the Alexander Technique
(CANSTAT)**
1472 East St. Joseph Boulevard
Apt No. 4
Montreal
Tel: 1 416 631 8127
Fax: 1 416 631 0094
email: fajin@cam.org

**Centre D'Analisi
Psico-Corporal (APTAE)**
c/o Nàpols 338 Esc. Drt 6* 4a
08025 Barcelona
Tel: 34 3 207 6516
Fax: 34 3 438 4827
email: xaviortiz@ms3.redestb.es

The Constructive Teaching Centre
18 Lansdowne Road
London W11
Tel: 44 207 727 7222

Danish Society of Teachers of the Alexander Technique (DFLAT)
Amager Faelledvej 4
DK 2300
Copenhagen 5
Denmark
Tel: 45 32 96 20 19
Fax: 45 32 96 20 39
email: dflat@post4.tele.dk

Eutokia Birth Centre
5 Milman Road
London NW6 6EN
Tel: 44 208 969 5356
email: moshe.machover@kcl.ac.uk

German Society of Teachers of the Alexander Technique (GLAT)
Postfach 5312
79020 Freiburg
Germany
Tel & Fax: 49 761 383 357
email: glat@tonline.de

Israeli Society of Teachers of the Alexander Technique ((ISTAT)
PO Box 715
Karkur 37106
Israel
Tel: 972 6 378 244
Fax: 972 6 272 211
email: daliax@netvision.net.i

London Academy of Music and Dramatic Art
226 Cromwell Road
London SW5 0SR
Tel: 44 207 373 9883
http://www.lamda.org.uk
email: enquiries@lamda.org.uk

Netherlands Society of Teachers of the Alexander Technique (NeVLAT)
Postbus 15591
1001 NB Amsterdam
The Netherlands
Tel: 31 20 625 3163

The Society of Teachers of the Alexander Technique (STAT)
20 London House
266 Fulham Road
London SW10 9EL
Tel: 44 207 351 0828
email: info@stat.org.uk

STAT books
Tel: 44 207 352 0666
email: statbooks@stat.org.uk

South African Society of Teachers of the Alexander Technique (SASTAT)
17 Ash Street
Observatory 7925
South Africa
Tel & Fax: 27 21 439 3440
email: ingridw@iafrica.com

Schweizerischer Verband der Lehrerinnen und Lehrer der F. M. Alexander-Technik
(SVLAT)
Postfach
CH 8032 Zürich
Switzerland
Tel: 41 1 201 03 43
email: info@svlat.ch

INSTITUTIONS USING THE ALEXANDER TECHNIQUE

The Alexander Technique is useful for a variety of performance-based activities; here are just some of the prestigious institutions which use the Technique on a regular basis.

Academy of Music, San Sebastian, Spain

Amadeus International Business Consultants, London, UK

Beer Davis Publicity Consultants, London, UK

Boston University School for the Arts, Boston, Maine, USA

Bremen Opera, Germany

Bristol Old Vic Theatre School, Bristol, UK

British Association for Performing Arts Medicine

Central School of Speech and Drama, London, UK

Cheltenham Ladies' College, Cheltenham, UK

Dramaten Teatre, Stockholm, Sweden

Estonia Academy of Music and Drama, Tallinn, Estonia

Eton College, UK

Ferens Voice Clinic, Middlesex Hospital, UK

Glaxo Wellcome Foundation, London, UK

Guildford Drama School, Guildford, Surrey, UK

Guildhall School of Music and Drama, London, UK

Indiana University, USA

Juilliard School, New York, USA

London Academy of Music and Dramatic Art, London, UK

Metropolitan Opera, New York, USA

Mountview Theatre School, London, UK

New England Conservatory of Music, USA

New York University, USA

Nimrod Theatre, Sydney, Australia

Northwestern University School of Music and School of Speech, Australia

Purcell School, London, UK

Rogaland Theatre, Stavanger, Norway

Royal Academy of Dramatic Art, London, UK

Royal Academy of Music, London, UK

Royal College of Music, London, UK

Royal National Theatre, London, UK

Royal Northern College of Music, Manchester, UK

Shakespeare's Globe Theatre, London, UK

Sotheby's Auctioneers, London, UK

State Theatre School, Oslo, Norway

The Actor's Centre, Dublin, Ireland

The Actor's Studio, New York, USA

The American Academy of Dramatic Arts, New York, USA

The Aspen Music Festival and School, Colorado, USA

The Eastman School of Music, Rochester, NY

The London Philharmonic, London, UK

The Menuhin School, UK

The Royal Festival Hall, London, UK

Trondelag Theatre, Tronheim, Norway

Westminster Public School, London, UK

Yale University (drama department), Connecticut, USA

INDEX

ACKNOWLEDGEMENTS

The authors would like to thank the models *Nikki Amuka-Bird, Priyanga Elan, Dominic, Jack, Sam* and *Hermione Murray, Ryan Elsworthy, Kamal Thapen, Christine Baden-Semper* and her granddaugther *Maya Marriott-Semper*.

With thanks to *Michael Bloch* for writing the biography of F. M. Alexander, *Walter* and *Dilys Carrington* for their encouragement and generosity, *Jackie Loxton, Ruth Murray* and *Peggy Williams* for their unstinting help, *Guy Ryecart* and *Kate Heal* for their meticulous attention to detail. And with special thanks to *Glynn Macdonald* for love, inspiration and constant support.

PICTURE ACKNOWLEDGEMENTS

Every effort has been made to trace copyright holders and obtain permission. The publishers apologise for any omissions and would be pleased to make any necessary changes at subsequent printings

AKG, London 30b, 48l, 52, 169; **Bruce Coleman Collection** 51t; **Corbis** 50t, 51, 203t / Bettmann Archive 29, 193, 202, 212-213 / Hulton Getty 172, 208 / Wolfgang Kaehler 182b / Catherine Karnow 198 / Mike King 46l; **Tony Stone Images** 26b, 27b, 43r, 46r, 50b, 58, 59tr, 62, 63t, 63b, 175t, 190, 194, 196, 207t, 208, 211tr.